FRO...
WALKING TOURS

MONTREAL &
QUEBEC CITY

BY
ALICE GARRARD

PRENTICE HALL TRAVEL

NEW YORK • LONDON • TORONTO • SYDNEY
TOKYO • SINGAPORE

FROMMER BOOKS
Published by Prentice Hall Reference
15 Columbus Circle
New York, NY 10023

Library of Congress Cataloging-in-Publication Data

Garrard, Alice.
Frommer's Walking Tours: Montréal & Québec City/by Alice Garrard.
    p.   c.m.—(Frommer's walking tours)
Includes index.
ISBN 0-671-88504-9 : $12.00
1. Montréal (Québec)—Tours. 2. Québec (Québec)—Tours. 3. Walking—
Québec (Province)—Montréal—Guidebooks. 4. Walking—Québec
(Province)—Québec—Guidebooks. I. Title. II. Title: Montréal and Qué-
bec City. III. Series.
F1054.5.M83G36   1994   94-4359
917.14′2804647—dc20   CIP

Design by Robert Bull Design
Maps by Ortelius Design

FROMMER'S EDITORIAL STAFF

Vice President/Editorial Director: Marilyn Wood
Executive Editor: Alice Fellows
Senior Editor: Lisa Renaud
Editors: Charlotte Allstrom, Margaret Bowen, Thomas F. Hirsch, Peter
    Katucki, Theodore Stavrou, Alice Thompson
Assistant Editors: Ian Wilker, Douglas Stallings
Managing Editor: Leanne Coupe

CONTENTS

Introducing Montréal & Québec City   1

The Walking Tours

Montréal
1 Old Montréal   11
2 Old Port & Lachine Canal   25
3 Olympic Park & the Botanical Garden   35
4 Mont-Royal   45
5 Downtown Montréal   53
6 A Modern Architecture Tour   61
7 A Shopper's Walk   73
8 Ile Ste-Hélène & Ile Notre-Dame   85
9 Plateau Mont-Royal   95
10 Ethnic Montréal   101

Québec City
11 Upper Town   109
12 The Grande Allée & Battlefields Park   121
13 Lower Town & Old Port   135

Essentials
   Getting to Know Montréal   149
   Getting to Know Québec City   155
   Recommended Reading   159

Index   162

LIST OF MAPS

Eastern Canada 3

Montréal
Old Montréal 13

Old Port & Lachine Canal 26–27

Olympic Park & the Botanical Garden 37

Mont-Royal 47

Downtown Montréal 55

A Modern Architecture Tour 63

A Shopper's Walk 75

Ile Ste-Hélène & Ile Notre-Dame 87

Plateau Mont-Royal 97

Ethnic Montréal 103

Montréal Metro 151

Québec City
Upper Town 111

The Grande Allée & Battlefields Park 122–123

Lower Town & Old Port 137

DEDICATION

To Gilles,
whose enthusiasm for Québec, and for life,
knows no bounds

ACKNOWLEDGMENTS

For their insights and assistance, I particularly want to thank Gilles Bengle of the Greater Montréal Convention and Tourism Bureau; Pierre Tougas of the Government of Québec Ministry of Tourism in Montréal; Maurice Boucher at the Canadian Centre for Architecture in Montréal; Brian LeCompte, Michael Banks, Daniel Soucy, Jean-Pierre Perrier, and Benoît Prieur in Montréal; Michel Gagnon, Mabel Wagner, and Sylvie Walter of the Greater Québec Area Tourism and Convention Bureau in Québec City; Monique Desprès, Charles Adlard, and Carole Turmel in Québec City; and Jean Buffard of the Délégation Générale du Québec in New York.

And for her expertise in transforming my manuscript and maps into a book, I especially want to thank my editor, Alice Thompson.

A SAFETY ADVISORY

Whenever you're traveling in an unfamiliar city or country, stay alert. Be aware of your immediate surroundings. Wear a moneybelt and keep a close eye on your possessions. Be particularly careful with cameras, purses, and wallets, all favorite targets of thieves and pickpockets.

INVITATION TO THE READERS

In researching this book, I have come across many wonderful finds, the best of which are included here. I'm sure that you will discover other appealing places as you explore Montréal and Québec City. Please don't keep them to yourself. Share your experiences, especially if you want to bring to my attention information that has changed since this book was researched. You can address your letters to:

Alice Garrard
Frommer's Walking Tours: Montréal & Québec City
Prentice Hall Travel
15 Columbus Circle
New York, NY 10023

Introducing Montréal & Québec City

Why is it that walkable cities, while so appealing, are all too rare? There's no better way to know a place than to stroll along its streets, through its architecture, and into its past. Happily, Montréal and Québec City are two of those unusual urban entities where exploring on foot is easy, fun, safe, and altogether rewarding.

In Montréal, with a population of 3 million in the greater urban area, an extensive metro system zips you from neighborhood to inviting neighborhood, and in compact Québec City, home to 465,000 in the greater urban area, you can walk everywhere without the aid of transport, though its steep hills may find you pausing to catch your breath from time to time.

Both cities are physically beautiful and your strolls through them will leave you with images of a vivid interplay of nature and architecture. In Montréal, a mountain audaciously pokes its head through the center of the city. Montréalers unabashedly love the "bump" on their landscape and climb on it much like puppies playing on a patient mother. Some of them rest eternally on it, since "the mountain," as it is known locally, is home to three of the city's cemeteries (Protestant, Catholic, and Jewish).

The topography of Québec City, which lies 166 miles northeast of

Montréal along the St. Lawrence River, is dominated by a dramatic promontory called Cap Diamant (Cape Diamond). Atop it lies a star-shaped citadel and a 100-year-old castlelike hotel with fairy-tale–inspired spires. Carefully preserved houses from the 17th and 18th centuries line slender, meandering streets.

So unique is Québec City visually and experientially, in fact, that Rudyard Kipling was moved to write in 1907: "Québec ranks by herself among those Mother-cities of whom none can say, 'This reminds me.'"

A WALK THROUGH HISTORY

NEW FRANCE, NEW FRONTIERS   Samuel de Champlain, armed with maps drawn by Jacques Cartier in 1535, arrived in North America with a crew of 28 men in 1608, determined to establish a French settlement at Québec. A year earlier, the Virginia Company had founded a fledgling colony called Jamestown hundreds of miles to the south. Champlain was successful, and by 1610 the fur trade upon which Canadian fortunes would be built had been established.

Champlain's fledgling settlement grew to become Québec's Lower Town, near the riverbank and beneath the cliffs of Cap Diamant. As you walk along the narrow streets today, you can almost hear the voices of those early merchants and traders, and see the boats gliding into the port.

But almost from the beginning there were attacks on Québec: first the Iroquois, then the English, and much later the Americans. Gradually the center of urban life moved to the top of the cliff—today the city's Upper Town—leaving the Lower Town to dwindle and become a wharf and warehouse area. To better defend themselves, the Québécois constructed a fortress atop the cape, which Jacques Cartier had called "the Gibraltar of the North" when he sailed past it in 1535. Its location at a *kebec,* an Algonquin word for "narrowing of the waters," was undeniably advantageous. But the Upper Town, as the Québécois were to discover, was not immune from attack either. In the 1750s the struggle between Britain and France had escalated, and strategic Québec had become a coveted prize.

COURAGE WAS FATAL TO THEM   The French sent 47-year-old Louis Joseph, Marquis de Montcalm, to command their forces in the town. To rout him, the British sent a fleet of ships carrying 8,500 men, under the command of a 32-year-old general named James Wolfe, who proceeded to lay siege to the city throughout the summer of 1759. But the French, entrenched atop Cap Diamant, held him at bay.

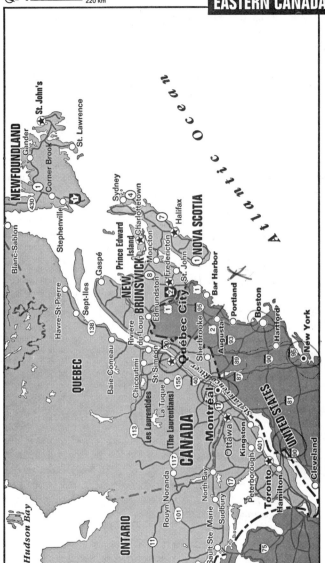

Then on the evening of September 12, Wolfe and 4,000 men rowed upriver to a cove behind the city. They silently—and remarkably—scaled the towering cliff face in darkness. The French lookouts, unable to see the troops in the dark, mistook them for the reinforcements they had been expecting and let them pass.

The ensuing battle for Québec, fought on the Plains of Abraham southwest of the Upper Town the next day, is one of the most famous in North American history. If you stand on the tranquil, grassy knoll today, it's easy to let your imagination drift back in time and visualize the short confrontation: The French and British square off a mere 40 yards apart. The French advance. The British shoot them down. The French advance again and are shot down again. And again. The battle ended in less than an hour, and the fate of Québec was sealed.

Both generals were mortally wounded in the battle. Wolfe lived just long enough to hear that he had won. When Montcalm, who died a few hours later, was told that he was dying, he replied, "All the better. I will not see the English in Québec." Today a memorial to both men overlooks Terrasse Dufferin (Dufferin Terrace) in Québec City; it is the only statue in the world commemorating both victor and vanquished of the same battle. The inscription, in neither French nor English but in Latin, says simply, "Courage was fatal to them."

The battle that took their lives broke the back of New France. It also broke its heart, but it did not diminish its spirit, which remains alive and well to this day. And while the French may have failed in North America as military strategists, they left an undying cultural legacy and outdid themselves in the area of explorations. Their far-ranging fur traders, navigators, and missionaries opened up not only Canada but most of the United States. At least 35 of the 50 states were either discovered, mapped, or settled by Frenchmen, who left behind some 4,000 place names to prove it, among them Detroit, St. Louis, New Orleans, Duluth, and Des Moines.

MEANWHILE IN MONTREAL . . .   In 1535 the French explorer Jacques Cartier, on the second of his voyages of exploration in the New World (he had discovered Newfoundland, the Magdalen Islands, and the Gaspé Peninsula the year before), got hung up at the rapids just west of a fairly large island in the St. Lawrence River. In a fit of optimism mingled with frustration, he bestowed on them the name "La Chine," or China, thinking that the rapids provided (or hindered) passage to the East.

Once disentangled from the rapids, Cartier disembarked on the island to have a look around. What he found was an Iroquois village, called Hochelaga, of about 50 wooden houses built in a circle at the base of a small mountain, which he called Mont-Royal. But Cartier's interests lay elsewhere, and a few days later he headed upriver. He would return to this part of the world, but not to the place that would become known as Montréal. Hochelaga would exist in peace for more than 100 years.

In 1642 (the year that Galileo died and Isaac Newton was born; 7

years after the death of Samuel de Champlain, the founder of Québec City; and 22 years after the *Mayflower* reached America and the first slaves were imported into Jamestown), Paul de Chomeday, Sieur de Maisonneuve, arrived to establish a colony and to plant a cross atop Mont-Royal. Maisonneuve and his band of settlers founded Ville-Marie, dedicated to the Virgin Mary, at the spot that is now place Royale in Old Montréal. They built a fort, a chapel, stores, and houses; and pioneer Jeanne Mance founded and named Hôtel-Dieu-de-Montréal hospital, which still exists today.

Life could not have been easy for the French settlers. The Iroquois did not choose to live in peace with them, unlike the friendly Algonquins in nearby regions. Maisonneuve had vowed he would settle the area "even if the very trees of the island turn to Iroquois." It must have seemed that way to the handful of inhabitants of Ville-Marie.

Fighting between the French and the Iroquois went on for a period of years, and the settlers were bolstered by the presence and prowess of such undauntable souls as la Salle, du Luth, la Mothe-Cadillac, and the brothers Lemoyne, all of whom later left their marks, and their names, on territories in the Great Lakes and Mississippi.

At place d'Armes stands a statue of Maisonneuve, marking the spot where the settlers finally defeated the Iroquois in bloody hand-to-hand fighting, with Maisonneuve himself locked in mortal combat with the Iroquois chief. Maisonneuve won.

After that victory, the settlement flourished for more than 100 years, particularly after 1654, when a boatload of young French women, known as the *filles du roi* (daughters of the king), arrived. They had been recruited from France to become the brides of the bachelor colonists. Increasingly, the settlement became known as Montréal.

Then animosities heated up between the French and the British, and in September 1760, Montréal fell to the British, a week shy of a year after General Wolfe's forces defeated those of General Montcalm on the Plains of Abraham in Québec City. Shortly afterward, General Thomas Gage, who became the first governor of Montréal under the British, commented that the inhabitants were "gay and sprightly . . . and from the number of silk robes, laced coats, and powdered heads of both sexes . . . perambulating in the streets from morning to night a stranger would be induced to believe Montréal is entirely inhabited by people of independent and plentiful fortunes."

It wasn't until the 1800s that Montréal, by then a "metropolis" of 3,500, outgrew the area now known as Old Montréal. Its ancient walls may no longer stand, but half of its long and colorful past is preserved in the picturesque streets, houses, and churches of the old city.

THE YANKEE BLITZ The capitulation of Québec and Montréal left Britain master of all North America down to the Mexican border. In 1763, in the Treaty of Paris, the king of France ceded all of Canada to the king of England. The British called the territory that included Québec City, Montréal, and a town called Trois Rivieres, Québec, and Benjamin Franklin, His Majesty's Postmaster General in the British colonies of North America, set up mail service in all three towns.

The French soldiers returned to France, but the French people, and their language, remained in Québec. This Catholic people, who had lived here for more than two centuries, now had to make way for changes, including another religious group, the Protestants, mainly Anglicans.

In 1791, Canada was separated into two regions, roughly divided north and south by the Ottawa River: Lower Canada, or Québec, with Québec City as provincial capital; and Upper Canada, which would become Ontario. The British settlers tended to make their homes west of the Ottawa River. Half of Canada's population would remain French speaking until almost the mid-19th century (by 1990, that percentage had dropped to one-quarter).

A quirk of history, Britain's victory over France in America ultimately led to its worst defeat. If the French had held onto Canada, the British government would surely have treated its American colonists more benevolently. As it was, it made the colonists pay for the outrageous costs of the French and Indian Wars, and slapped so many taxes on all imports—especially tea—that the infuriated colonists openly rebelled against the Crown.

But if the British misjudged the temper of the colonists, the Americans were equally wrong about the mood of the Canadians. George Washington felt sure that the French in the north would want to join the Revolution, or at least be supportive of it. He was mistaken on both counts. Even the persuasiveness of Benjamin Franklin, who came in person to argue the cause, failed to win them over. The plucky French had little love for either of the English-speaking antagonists, but they were staunch Royalists and devout Catholics, with no sympathy for the "godless" republicans to the south. Only a handful changed sides, and three of Washington's feistiest generals came to grief over the French resistance: the daredevil Vermonter Ethan Allen and his Green Mountain Boys were taken prisoner at Montréal; General Richard Montgomery fell in Québec; and ambitious Colonel Benedict Arnold was driven back in defeat.

During the War of 1812—the same year that James Madison became president of the United States and Louisiana became a state—another U.S. Army marched into Québec. Again the French sided with the British and repulsed the invaders. The war ended in a draw, but with some positive results. Britain and the young United States agreed to demilitarize the Great Lakes and to extend their mutual border along the 49th Parallel to the Rockies.

The province of Québec was incorporated in 1832 and received its charter in 1840. In 1867, the British North America Act created the federation of four provinces: Québec, Ontario, Nova Scotia, and New Brunswick.

MODERN TIMES   Québec City seems to have changed little over time, which is a large part of its appeal. The ancient walls that have protected it for almost four centuries still stand, preserving for posterity the heart of New France. In acknowledgment of this, UNESCO bestowed World Heritage Site status on Québec City in 1985, the only North American city to be so honored.

Montréal, on the other hand, while cradling its own history in Old Montréal, has gone through an urban metamorphosis. During the Prohibition era, Montréal was "wet" when the United States was "dry." Colorful imbibers from the States flocked to this large city so conveniently close to the American border, and mixed with the rowdy elements from the port, much to the distress of Montréal's mainly upstanding citizenry. They remained distressed for half a century, but in the 1950s a cleanup began, followed in the 1960s and beyond by ambitious building and expansion that have made Montréal the vibrant metropolis it is today.

In 1962, the city's first skyscraper, place Ville-Marie, rose on the urban landscape and spurred a renaissance of the downtown area; that same year, Montréal welcomed 53 million people to the international Expo '67; and in 1976, 59 million people thronged here to witness the Olympic Games.

The gleaming skyscrapers, the towering hotels, and the highly practical Underground City, so much a part of modern Montréal, date mostly from the last 30 years. And linking them all together is an efficient metro system, completed in 1966 and extended in 1988, with 65 stations covering more than 40 miles.

Québec's products and personalities have played a visible part in international contemporary culture. Consider Seagrams whisky, Molson beer, the Ski-Doo (Joseph-Armand Bombardier invented the first snowmobile in the late 1950s); the music of Leonard Cohen, Celine Dion, and Oscar Peterson; and the acting of Norma Shearer, Genevieve Bujold, Glenn Ford, and William Shatner.

The Canadiens, Montréal's famous ice-hockey team, was founded in 1909 and has gone on to win more world championships than any other professional team, creating star athletes like Guy Lafleur and Maurice "the Rocket" Richard and his brother Henri (the "Pocket Rocket") along the way. And Montréal was the first city outside the United States to be awarded a major-league baseball franchise, the Montréal Expos, who played their first game in 1969.

A BILINGUAL EXPERIENCE

Although more than 200 years have passed since French troops withdrew from Québec, it remains a delightfully, determinedly French province. Montréal's population is 66% French speaking, while Québec City's is 95% French speaking, and a visit to either city promises the kind of cultural experience most people have to go to Europe to get.

If your French-language skills are shaky, don't worry that you'll run into a linguistic stone wall here. Montréal may be the largest French-speaking city outside of Paris, but most Montréalers grow up speaking both French and English, switching impressively and graciously from one language to the other as the situation demands.

While fewer people in Québec City speak English as comfortably or as fluently as those in Montréal (which makes it an even better place to practice your French), everyone is friendly and helpful, and people who work in hotels, restaurants, and tourist attractions are used to speaking English. Typically, those who claim to know very little English will go on to impress you with their command of the language.

So while you soak up Québec's culture, relive its unique history, and get to know the lay of the land in Montréal and Québec City, remember that walking—neighborhood by neighborhood—is the best way to make the acquaintance of these two fun, fascinating cities. "Je Me Souviens," the motto of the province of Québec, means "I remember," and any sojourner here is bound to remember the myriad experiences that unfold every step of the way.

MONTREAL

Old Montréal

Start: Eglise Notre-Dame-de-Bonsecours.
Finish: Musée Marc-Aurele Fortin.
Time: 2 to 3 hours.
Metro: Champ-de-Mars; follow the signs to Vieux-Montréal (Old Montréal).
Best Time: Anytime. Old Montréal is lively (and safe) day or night, but if you are a museum-goer, avoid Mondays, when some of the museums are closed. On weekends and holidays, Montréalers will be here in full force, enjoying the plazas, the architecture, and ambience of the oldest, most charming part of their city.

Of all the neighborhoods in Montréal, this, the oldest one, is perhaps dearest to everyone's heart. After all, the city was born here, in 1642, by the river at Pointe-à-Callière. It is the historical and sentimental heart of the city, and its museums, churches, shops, restaurants, cafés, and waterfront park will keep you enthralled for hours.

Old Montréal is larger than you might think, bounded on the north by rue St-Jacques, once the "Wall Street" of Montréal and still home to many banks; to the south by the St. Lawrence River, the Old Port, and rue de la Commune; to the east by rue Berri; and to the west by rue McGill.

To start this tour, go to the Champ-de-Mars metro station, which takes its name from the former parade ground, now a public space, behind the City Hall. (Just north of the metro, and not included on this walk, is the city's small but colorful Chinatown, centered on pedestrian rues de la Gauchetière and Clark; you might want to visit it later.) When you exit the metro, watch for signs for "Vieux-Montréal" and follow rue Bonsecours up the hill. Continue along Bonsecours several blocks until you reach rue St-Paul, the oldest thoroughfare in Montréal (1672), on which stands the diminutive:

1. **Eglise Notre-Dame-de-Bonsecours** (1673), or Sailors' Church. The church was founded in 1657 by Marguerite Bourgeoys, a nun and teacher who was made a saint in 1982. A small museum dedicated to her is downstairs and features the story of her life and work in 58 small scenes. Sailors have historically made pilgrimages to the church to give thanks for being saved at sea. Climb up to the tower for a memorable view of the harbor and the Old Town.

Right across rue St-Paul from the church, at no. 401, is a house that offers a look at what life was like in Montréal in the late 18th century. The:

2. **Maison Calvet** (Calvet House) was built in 1725 and restored from 1964 to 1966. You won't find authentic furnishings inside—it's now a gourmet food shop—but in the old days such a house would have been inhabited by some fairly well-to-do Montréalers. Pierre du Calvet, believed to be the house's original owner, was a French Huguenot who supported the American Revolution. Calvet met with Benjamin Franklin in Montréal in 1775, and was imprisoned from 1780 to 1783 for supplying money to the Americans.

The house, with a typical sloped roof to discourage snow buildup, is constructed of Montréal graystone.

Just beyond the Sailor's Church, heading west down rue St-Paul, is an imposing building with a colonnaded facade and handsome dome, the graystone:

3. **Marché Bonsecours** (Bonsecours Market). Built between 1845 and 1852, it was first used as the City Hall, then the central market (one market day each week was held in place Jacques-Cartier, and the rest of the week market activities took place here), and later the home of the municipality's housing and planning offices.

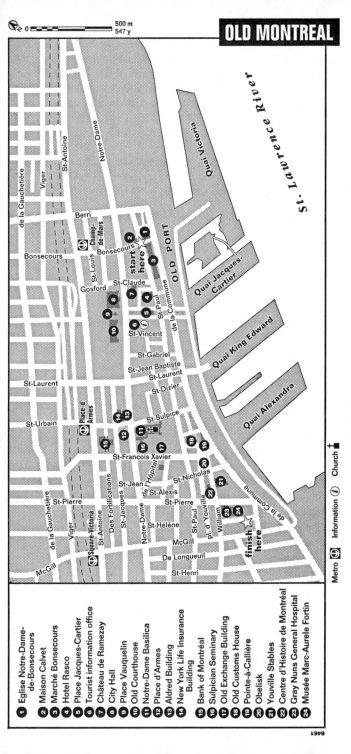

OLD MONTREAL

St. Lawrence River

Quai Victoria

Quai Jacques-Cartier

Quai King Edward

Quai Alexandra

OLD PORT

de la Commune

0 — 500 m
547 y

Metro Ⓜ Information ⓘ Church ✝

start here

finish here

1 Eglise Notre-Dame-de-Bonsecours
2 Maison Calvet
3 Marché Bonsecours
4 Hotel Rasco
5 Place Jacques-Cartier
6 Tourist information office
7 Château de Ramezay
8 City Hall
9 Place Vauquelin
10 Old Courthouse
11 Notre-Dame Basilica
12 Place d'Armes
13 Aldred Building
14 New York Life Insurance Building
15 Bank of Montréal
16 Sulpician Seminary
17 Old Exchange Building
18 Old Customs House
19 Pointe-à-Callière
20 Obelisk
21 Youville Stables
22 Centre d'Histoire de Montréal
23 Gray Nuns General Hospital
24 Musée Marc-Aurele Fortin

6461

The building was restored in 1964 and again in 1992. In 1992, it served as the information and exhibition center for the city's five-month-long 350th birthday celebration, and the following year housed a major exhibition on Alexander the Great. Hopefully it will continue to be used by the city in similar capacities.

When the Bonsecours Market was first built, the dome could be seen from everywhere in the city. The Doric columns that add to the building's distinctiveness were cast in England, and the prominent silver dome has long served as a landmark for seafarers coming into the harbor.

Continue down rue St-Paul. At no. 281 you'll see the former:

4. **Hotel Rasco,** built in 1836 for Francisco Rasco, an Italian who came to Canada to manage a hotel for the Molson family. Soon he became successful with his own hotel. The 150-room Rasco was the Ritz of its day in Montréal, hosting the great and famous. Guests included Charles Dickens and his wife, who stayed here in 1842 when Dickens was directing some of his plays at the theater across the street.

The hotel lives on in legend if not in fact, devoid of its original striking architectural detail. Rasco left in 1844, and the hotel slipped into decline. Between 1960 and 1981 it stood empty, but the city took it over and restored it in 1982. It now houses city offices.

Continue along rue St-Paul one more block to arrive at the focus of summer activity in Old Montréal—and, indeed, a magnet for people year-round:

5. **place Jacques-Cartier,** which opened as a marketplace in 1804. Without a doubt the most enchanting of the Old City's squares, its cobbled streets, gentle downhill slope, ancient buildings, and horse-drawn carriages transport you back in time, while outdoor cafés, street entertainers, itinerant artists, and flower vendors invite you to linger. Everyone seems to gravitate to the square on nice days to enjoy the circus of activity here. Calèches depart from the southern end of the square for horse-drawn tours of Old Montréal.

At the northern end of place Jacques-Cartier looms the monument to Lord Horatio Nelson, hero of Trafalgar, erected in 1809. As you make your way toward it, take time to notice the old buildings that cradle place Jacques-Cartier. Plaques in French and English will tell you about some of them: the Vandelac House (no. 433), the del Vecchio House (nos. 404 to 410), and the Cartier House (no. 407). These early houses were well suited to the rigors of life in the fledgling town of Montréal: Steep roofs

FEMALE PIONEERS

Montréal has always honored its female movers and shakers, as various monuments around the city attest. Three remarkable women made their mark on the city in the first 100 years of its existence.

Jeanne Mance

Montréal's first secular nurse, Jeanne Mance (1606–1673) arrived with Maisonneuve in 1653 and did so much to keep the fledgling colony afloat that some consider her a co-founder of Ville-Marie. Mance established the city's first hospital, called Hôtel Dieu but referred to as "la maison de Mlle. Mance." Like Maisonneuve, Mance was from the Champagne region of France, and she probably got her experience as a nurse in the hospital in her home town of Langres during the Thirty Years War.

Marguerite Bourgeoys

Montréal's first teacher, Marguerite Bourgeoys (1620–1700) was a nun who arrived in Ville-Marie in 1653, just after Jeanne Mance. She founded the first Canadian religious order, a teaching order called Congregation Notre Dame, and, in 1658, the first school for young women, which first operated out of a stable. Bourgeoys was canonized by Pope John Paul II in 1982.

Marguerite d'Youville

Unlike Jeanne Mance and Marguerite Bourgeoys, Marguerite d'Youville (1701–1771) was born in Québec. D'Youville was married in 1722 and widowed in 1730. In 1737, she founded the Congregation of Sisters of Charity, better known as the Gray Nuns. Following in the footsteps of Jeanne Mance, she administered Ville-Marie's second hospital, the Hôpital Général, built in 1694. The Sisters of Charity were established in Québec City in 1849. Marguerite d'Youville was canonized by Pope John Paul II in 1990, making her the first Canadian-born saint.

shed the heavy winter snows rather than break under the burden, and small windows with double casements let in light while keeping out wintry breezes and hostile arrows; when shuttered, the windows were almost as effective as the heavy stone walls in fending off attacks or the antics of devil-may-care trappers fresh from an evening's imbibing in nearby taverns.

REFUELING STOP   Some of the old buildings in and around place Jacques-Cartier harbor fine restaurants and cafés. Try to find a seat in **La Maison Cartier** (no. 407), on the east side of the square near the bottom of the hill. Sit in the courtyard in warm weather—there might be live music—or the terrace overlooking the activity of the square.

To the left of the square, across rue St-Vincent on rue Notre-Dame, is a small but dependably helpful:

6. **tourist information office,** where you may collect brochures and maps or ask questions of the bilingual staff. On this site once stood the famed Silver Dollar Saloon, long since torn down. The drinking place got its name and renown from 350 silver dollars embedded in its floor.

On the other side of place Jacques-Cartier, on rue Notre-Dame, is the:

7. **Château de Ramezay,** built by Claude de Ramezay between 1705 and 1706 in the French Regime style typical of the period. This was the home of the city's royal French governors, starting with de Ramezay, for four decades before being taken over and used for the same purpose by the British.

In 1775 an army of American "rebels" invaded and held Montréal, using the château as their headquarters. Benjamin Franklin, sent to persuade Montréalers to rise with the colonists against British rule, stayed in the château but failed to sway Québec's leaders to join his cause.

The house has had other uses over the years. It was a courthouse, government office building, teachers' college, and headquarters for Laval University before becoming a museum in 1895. Inside are furnishings, tools, oil paintings, costumes, and other objects related to the economic and social activities of the 18th century and the first half of the 19th century.

Across rue Notre-Dame from the Château Ramezay stands the impressive Second Empire–style:

8. **City Hall,** built between 1872 and 1878. The city's administrative office moved here from the second floor of Bonsecours Market, where they had been for 25 years. In 1922 the building barely survived a disastrous fire; only the exterior walls re-

mained, and after tremendous rebuilding and the addition of another floor it reopened in 1926.

Take a minute to look inside at the generous use of Italian marble and the French art deco lamps and bronze-and-glass chandelier. The sculptures at the entry are *Woman with a Pail* and *The Sower,* both by Alfred Laliberté.

Alongside City Hall is:

9. place Vauquelin, a public square since 1858, with a splashing fountain and view of Champ-de-Mars. It takes its name from Jean Vauquelin, commander of the French fleet in New France. Beside place Vauquelin stands the imposing domed:

10. Old Court House, most of which was built in 1856 although the third floor and dome were added in 1891. The Organizing Committee for the 1976 Olympic Games resided here, and the city's civil cases continued to be tried here until a new court house, the Palais de Justice, was built next door in 1978. Civic departments for the city of Montréal are housed here now. The statue beside the Old Court House, called *Hommage to Marguerite Bourgeoys,* is by sculptor Jules LaSalle.

Continue along rue Notre-Dame 5 blocks, crossing rue St-Sulpice, to the magnificent Neo-Gothic:

11. Notre-Dame Basilica (1829), designed by an Irishman living in New York named James O'Donnell. O'Donnell later converted to Roman Catholicism and is one of only a few people buried here. The main altar is made from a hand-carved linden tree. Behind the altar is the Chapel of the Sacred Heart (1982), a perennially popular choice for weddings. The chapel's altar, 32 bronze panels by Montréal artist Charles Daudelin, represents birth, life, and death. The church can seat 3,500 people, and its bell, one of the largest in North America, weighs 12 tons.

There is a small museum (open only on Saturday and Sunday) beside the chapel.

The basilica faces:

12. place d'Armes, created in the late 17th century and often the site of military celebrations. The centerpiece of the square is a monument to city founder and first governor, Paul de Chomeday, Sieur de Maisonneuve (1612–1676). Erected in 1895, it marks the spot (or close to it) where the settlers defeated the Iroquois warriors in bloody hand-to-hand fighting, with Maisonneuve himself locked in mortal combat with the Iroquois chief. Maisonneuve won, and lived here for 23 years.

The figures at the base of the monument represent three founders of Montréal—Charles Lemoyne (1626–1685), a farmer; Jeanne Mance, the founder of the first hospital in Montréal;

and Raphael-Lambert Closse, a soldier and the mayor of Ville-Marie—and an Iroquois warrior. Closse is depicted with his dog, Pilote, whose trusty bark once warned the early settlers of an impending Iroquois attack.

The monument is 30 feet (9 meters) tall; the statue of Maisonneuve alone, 13 feet (4 meters). The inscription reads "You are the buckwheat seed which will grow and multiply and spread throughout the country." The monument has been restored several times, most recently in 1991.

In the 17th century, the square was wedged between two cemeteries, one to the north and one to the south, causing it to be nicknamed "God's Acre." At this time, the village of Montréal, with the exception of a handful of houses, extended no farther north than rue St-Paul.

At place d'Armes in 1775, the American general Richard Montgomery presented arms when he and his troops captured Montréal during the American Revolutionary War. (Montgomery would be killed on New Year's Day of the same year in an unsuccessful siege of Québec City, which he co-led with the then-patriotic American Benedict Arnold.) A statue of King George III used to stand in the center of the square, but in 1775 Americans covered it with tar, and it later mysteriously disappeared (an early incident of vandalism).

Opposite the square and cater-corner to the basilica is the 23-story art deco:

13. Aldred Building, reminiscent of New York City's Empire State Building. The original plan, inspired by a proposal Eliel Saarinen did for a Chicago Tribune competition that was exhibited in Montréal in 1923, was for a 12-story building, but by the time it was completed in 1931, another 11 stories had been added. The building's original tenant was Aldred and Co. Ltd., a New York–based multinational finance company with offices in New York, London, and Paris. Even though the building is taller than its neighbors, it still coexists harmoniously with the architecture around the square.

Beside it stands the eight-story, red-sandstone:

14. New York Life Insurance Building, 511 place d'Armes, with its striking wrought-iron door and clock tower. Built in 1889, this was Montréal's first skyscraper, and it was equipped with a modern marvel, an elevator.

Directly across the square from the statue of Maisonneuve and the basilica is the domed, colonnaded:

15. Bank of Montréal, 119 rue St-Jacques, Montréal's oldest bank building (1847). Besides being impressive to look at outside and inside, it houses a small banking museum that shows what its early operations were like; admission is free.

From 1901 to 1905, the American architect Stanford White was in charge of extending the original building beyond Fortifications Lane to what is now rue St-Antoine. In this enlarged space he created a stunning banking chamber with high, green-marble columns topped with golden capitals; go inside and have a look at this still-splendid space. During this time, the cupola that had been removed in 1859 was rebuilt with a Roman basilica as the model. It was restored in 1988.

Opposite the square from the bank and adjacent to the basilica on rue Notre-Dame is the:

16. **Sulpician Seminary,** Montréal's oldest building and one that is surrounded by its oldest stone walls. It was erected by the Sulpician priests in 1658, a year after they arrived in Ville-Marie. The Sulpicians are part of the Order of Saint Sulpice, founded in Paris by Jean-Jacques Olier in 1641.

The building and a French garden in back, installed in 1666, are still used by the Sulpicians today. The clock on the facade dates from 1701 and has a movement made almost entirely of wood. Unfortunately the seminary is not open to the public.

REFUELING STOP I always manage to get hungry at place d'Armes, which is unfortunately a 10-minute walk from my favorite Old Montréal eateries. But I've discovered a place that's good for a rest break and a quick bite: the **Sorosa** restaurant at 407 rue Notre-Dame ouest; if you order food, choose pizza over pasta.

Walk past the Sulpician Seminary, heading west on rue Notre-Dame, and turn left at rue St-François-Xavier. At rue de l'hôpital, to your left, is the stately:

17. **Old Exchange Building,** which now houses the Centaur Theater, the city's only English-language theater. The beaux arts architecture is interesting in that the two entrances are on either side rather than in the center of the facade. The building, erected in 1903, was designed by the American architect George Post, who had just designed the New York Stock Exchange. It served as the city's stock exchange until 1965, and in 1966 was redesigned as a theater with two stages.

Continue down St-François Xavier; at rue St-Paul, turn left. L'Air du Temps, one of the city's oldest and most enduring jazz clubs, is on the corner, at no. 191. Walk the short distance to 150 rue St-Paul and the neoclassical:

18. Old Customs House (1836–1838). The building's original size was doubled in 1882 to what you see today by dismantling the southern wall, extending the building to the south, then reassembling the wall (much like the western facade of the Capitol in Washington, D.C.); walk around to the other side of the building for a look.

The Old Customs House faces the north side of place Royale, the first public square in the early settlement of Ville-Marie. Europeans and Amerindians used to come here to trade their wares.

Cross place D'Youville to the modern, triangular:

19. Pointe-à-Callière, which houses the Museum of Archaeology and History. It is the repository of treasures unearthed after more than 10 years of excavation here, the site where Montréal (Ville-Marie) was founded in 1642. The museum also incorporates, via an underground connection, the Old Customs House that you just saw.

A fort stood on this spot in 1645, and 30 years later, the château of a monsieur de Callière, from which the building and triangular square take their names. At that time, the St. Pierre River separated this piece of land from the mainland; it was made a canal in the 19th century and later filled in.

On the second floor of the modern building is a pleasant café (see Refueling Stop below), and just above that, a lookout with excellent views of the Old Port; the Old City; the harbor; Cité du Havre; and Habitat 67, designed by McGill College graduate Moshe Safdie for Expo '67.

The 354 prefabricated concrete boxes of Habitat 67, which weigh 85 tons each and were set in place by giant cranes, are connected by pedestrian walkways. They form 158 dwellings stacked into three pyramids. As you gaze out at the complex, imagine what a thrill it must be to live in one of these modern apartments and gaze out at the skyline of Old Montréal.

REFUELING STOP It's easy to visit the casual, second-floor **L'Arrivage** café when you're at Pointe-à-Callière. The view from here couldn't be pleasanter, and it's usually fine with the staff if you simply sit and sip a cup of coffee. Food is available, too, and the restaurant is open the same hours as the museum.

For a moderately priced French meal, try intimate, nearby

Bourlinguer, at 363 St-François-Xavier (closed Sunday). For hearty Polish fare, visit the **Stash Café** at 200 rue St-Paul ouest and rue St-François-Xavier.

At the back of Pointe-à-Callière, near rue St-François Xavier, stands an:

20. obelisk commemorating the founding of the city of Ville-Marie on May 18, 1642. The obelisk was erected here in 1893 by the Montréal Historical Society and bears the names of the city's early pioneers, including Maisonneuve and Mance.

Continuing west from the obelisk 2 blocks brings you to:

21. Youville Stables, on the left at 296–316 place d'Youville. The rooms within the iron-gated compound were built in 1825 on land owned by the Gray Nuns and were inspired by French commercial architecture. They were used mainly as warehouses.

Like much of the waterfront area, Youville "Stables" (the actual stables, next door, were made of wood and disappeared long ago) was run-down and forgotten until the 1960s, when a group of enterprising businesspeople decided to buy and renovate the property. Today the compound is an upscale office and dining area. Go inside the courtyard and take a look if the gates are open, and they usually are.

MOSHE SAFDIE

Born in Israel in 1938 and raised on a kibbutz until he was 16, Moshe Safdie moved to Montréal with his family and studied architecture at McGill University. Since that time he has done much to shape the architecture of Montréal, as well as that of Québec City, other parts of Canada, and the United States.

In 1963 Safdie designed the general plan for Expo '67, including Habitat 67, which was based on concepts in his McGill thesis. At that time, the 29-year-old Safdie was heralded by the London *Sunday Times* as the "heir to Le Corbusier." In 1991 Safdie completed the modern annex for the Musée des Beaux-Arts in Montréal; he has also designed the Museum of Civilization in Québec City and the National Gallery of Canada in Ottawa. Safdie, now based in Boston, Massachusetts, has taught at Harvard and Yale.

Continue another block west to 335 rue St-Pierre and the Dutch-style:

22. Centre d'Histoire de Montréal (Montréal History Center). Built in 1903 as Montréal's Central Fire Station, it now houses exhibits, including many audiovisual ones, about the city's past and present. Visitors learn about the early routes of exploration, the fur trade, architecture, public squares, the railroad, and life in Montréal from 1920 to 1950. There's even a simulated ride on a Montréal metro.

Compare this building's architecture, which is unusual in Montréal, with the simpler architecture around it. Prior to the erection of the Fire Station, the Ste-Anne Market stood on this site in the 19th century, followed by a Canadian Parliament building.

Less than a block away, at 138 rue St-Pierre, you'll pass the former:

23. Gray Nuns General Hospital, in operation from 1693 to 1851 and now the administrative offices and a novitiate for future nuns. Officially known as the Sisters of Charity of Montréal, the order was founded by the widow Marguerite d'Youville in 1737.

The building that you see, which incorporates several additions, was part of the city's General Hospital, run by the Charon Brothers but administered by d'Youville, who died here in 1771 (the wing in which she died was restored in 1980). The wall of the original chapel remains. Visits inside must be arranged in advance.

From here, look down rue St-Pierre for the brown awning at no. 118 that marks the entrance to the:

24. Musée Marc-Aurele Fortin, the only museum in the city devoted to a single Canadian artist. Fortin, who died in 1972, was well known for his renderings of Montréal and the Québec countryside, including Charlevoix and the Laurentian Mountains. His elms are particularly well-known (like Van Gogh's sunflowers) and are reminiscent of the time when giant Dutch elms lined rues Sherbrooke and St-Joseph in Montréal, before blight decimated them.

The museum charges an admission fee, but if you don't want to tour it, you could peek in the entrance and get a sense of Marc-Aurele Fortin's distinctive style (he first painted his canvases black before creating scenes on them) from the postcards sold in the reception area. Like far too many artists, Fortin did not achieve monetary success in his lifetime.

The museum is the final stop on this walking tour, and from

here you can cross rue de la Commune and the railroad tracks to explore Montréal's revitalized Old Port (to the left) or walk along the Lachine Canal (to the right); for both, see "Walking Tour 2—Old Port and Lachine Canal." You can also take the nearby Victoria metro to get to your next destination, or relax at a nearby eatery.

REFUELING STOP   For a snack in an informal atmosphere, and a trip down memory lane, go to **Il Etait Une Fois . . .** (Once Upon a Time), at 600 rue d'Youville at McGill. This memorabilia-filled café is housed in an old brick train station in use from 1909 to 1955 when there was train service between Montréal and Granby. You can get burgers, fish-and-chips, lobster rolls, malteds, and pie à la mode at this dependably filling place.

Old Port & Lachine Canal

Start: Quai Jacques-Cartier.
Finish: Atwater Market and the antiques district.
Time: 3 to 4 hours (2 hours if you choose not to walk along the canal).
Metro: Champ-de-Mars.
Best Time: The Old Port is best seen and experienced during the day, particularly a warm, sunny one. You can start out mid- to late afternoon on a Thursday or Friday because the Atwater Market, at the end of the canal part of the walk, stays open until 9pm on those nights.

The Old Port of Montréal has metamorphosed from a busy commercial area to a waterfront park, designed by Montréal-based architect Peter Rose and stretching from Berri to McGill streets. The park contains walkways, an artificial pond replacing old railway lines, two skating rinks in winter, and stunning views of the Old City year-round.

The revitalized waterfront now rivals "the mountain" as the favorite haunt of bikers, joggers, walkers, strollers, lovers, and lollers in good weather. Outdoor events and performances are also held

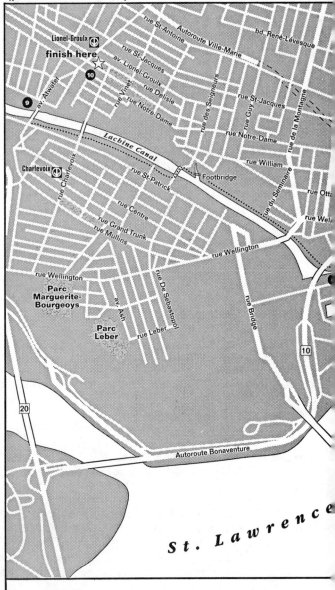

Scale: 0 — 1000 m / 1094 y

N

Lionel-Groulx

finish here

rue St-Antoine
Autoroute Ville-Marie
bd. René-Lévesque
rue St-Jacques
av. Lionel-Groulx
rue Delisle
rue Vinet
rue Notre-Dame
rue des Seigneurs
rue St-Jacques
rue Guy
rue de la Montagne
rue Notre-Dame
av. Atwater

Lachine Canal

Charlevoix

rue St-Patrick
rue William
Footbridge
rue du Séminaire
rue Otta
rue Wel

rue Charlevoix
rue Centre
rue Grand Trunk
rue Mullins
rue Wellington

rue Wellington

Parc Marguerite-Bourgeoys

Parc Leber

av. Ash
rue Leber
rue De Sebastopol
rue Bridge
20
10

Autoroute Bonaventure

St. Lawrence

① Quai Jacques-Cartier	⑥ Parc des Ecluses
② Bonsecours Basin Park	⑦ Lachine Canal
③ Quai de l' Horloge	⑧ Farine Five Roses
④ Quai King-Edward	⑨ Atwater Market
⑤ Quai Alexandra	⑩ Antiques district

6462

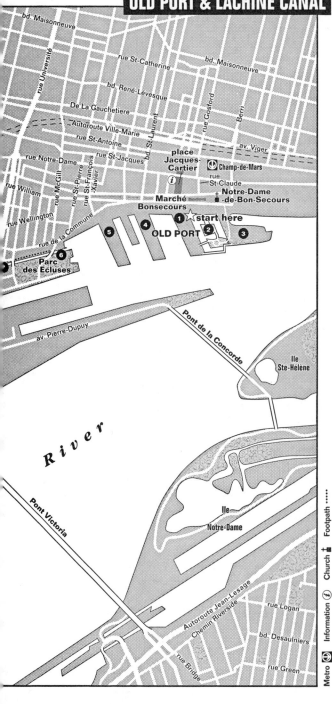

bd. Maisonneuve

rue St-Catherine

bd. Maisonneuve

bd. René-Lévesque

De La Gauchetiere

Autoroute Ville-Marie

rue St-Antoine

rue St-Jacques

rue Notre-Dame

rue William

rue Wellington

rue de la Commune

rue Université

rue St-Laurent

rue St-Pierre

rue St-François-Xavier

rue Gosford

Berri

av. Viger

place Jacques-Cartier

Champ-de-Mars

rue St-Claude

Notre-Dame-de-Bon-Secours

Marché Bonsecours

1 ☆ **start here**

2

3

OLD PORT

4

5

6 Parc des Écluses

rue McGill

av. Pierre-Dupuy

Pont de la Concorde

Île Ste-Hélène

River

Pont Victoria

Île Notre-Dame

Autoroute Jean-Lesage

Chemin Riverside

rue Logan

bd. Desaulniers

rue Bridge

rue Green

Metro ⊛ Information *i* Church † Footpath ·····

here. At the port, you can rent bicycles, four-wheeled bikes called *pédalos,* and rollerblades, or tour around in a trolley for a small fee. If you combine a stroll along the waterfront quays with a walk along the Lachine Canal, you'll have an invigorating outing indeed.

At the Old Port, start at the most logical place:

1. **Quai Jacques-Cartier,** opposite place Jacques-Cartier. The information center, in the Jacques Cartier Pavilion, is here, as is the pédalo (also known as "Q-cycle") rental stand—you'll see plenty of folks darting around the port in these four-wheel buggies.

   From Quai Jacques-Cartier (to the right of the information center, as you face it), you can grab the Aqua-Taxi to the landscaped park at Cité du Havre; ride the sleek, glass-roof Bateau-Mouche or the Croisière Nouvelle Orleans; get a boat to visit Ile Ste-Hélène and Ile Notre-Dame; or tour *Le Pelican,* a three-masted schooner (hopefully, it'll still be in port when you visit). Adjacent to these boats is the Port d'Escale marina, which can accommodate 95 boats.

   By all means, walk to the end of the quay; the view is great from there. You can see the geodesic dome and the Calder sculpture on Ile Ste-Hélène, a dramatic view of the skyline of Old Montréal, Jacques Cartier Bridge, La Ronde amusement park (site of fantastic fireworks in summer), Habitat 67 (though not the best view of it), the Molson brewery, and the clock tower.

   From the end of Quai Jacques-Cartier, you can follow walkways to the:

2. **Bonsecours Basin Park.** The park is located on a small island created from landfill to provide a play area and a pavilion. If you want to do some extensive exploring (you'll have to double back, mind you), follow the walkway to the:

3. **Quai de l'Horloge,** which has a distinctive clock tower at its end. The tower was erected to commemorate the fallen soldiers of World War I, and you can actually climb to the top, all 192 steps of it.

   If you've made the trek out to the clock tower, wend your way back to Quai Jacques-Cartier, and then continue along the waterfront promenade (Promenade du Vieux-Port) past it to the Old Port's next quay:

4. **Quai King-Edward,** which still has its original sheds, put to good use with temporary exhibitions and special summer

JOHN MOLSON & HIS LEGACY

Molson beer was first made on a hot July day in 1786 at a brewery founded by 23-year-old John Molson (1763–1836), who had immigrated to Montréal from England when he was 18. The oldest family business in Canada was established just east of Old Montréal on the corner of rues Papineau and Notre-Dame, where you'll find it today, more than 200 years later.

Beer was hard to come by in Montréal in the late 18th century, and, in fact, imported porter-style beer cost more than imported rum. In his first year of operation, Molson produced 80 hogsheads of ale, the equivalent of 53,000 bottles of beer.

Between 1838 and 1858, the brewery burned eight times, but it was always rebuilt immediately, bigger each time. Today Molson Breweries remains the oldest continuously active brewery in North America, and the original cellars are preserved inside the brewery walls.

When John Molson died in 1836 at age 73, his success extended far beyond the production of beer. He built Canada's first steamboat, in 1809, followed by about 10 more. (Until the 1850s, most of the immigrants to Montréal arrived by steamboat from Québec City.) In 1832, Molson funded Canada's first railway, the Champlain and St-Lawrence Railroad. He was also a founder of the Montréal General Hospital and served as chairman of the board of the Bank of Montréal. (His son William founded the Molson Bank in 1854, which merged with the Bank of Montréal in 1925.)

Molson Breweries, founded by an enterprising 23-year-old immigrant, donates almost $3 million to charity annually.

attractions. Here you'll discover a sprawling flea market on the lower level (admission is free) and Images du Futur, with changing exhibitions, on the upper level (there may be an admission fee). Across from them is an IMAX theater. You can also rent bicycles or get them repaired here.

Take a left as you leave the quay; on your right is a pond that lures people like a magnet on sunny days, especially those who have brought miniature boats to sail. You'll also find rest rooms here.

Across rue de la Commune is Pointe-à-Callière and the modern Museum of Archaeology and History (see "Walking Tour 1—Old Montréal"). If you're curious, you can peek into the ancient ruins of the city through the museum's sidewalk-level windows.

Opposite rue de Callière is:

5. **Quai Alexandra** and the Gare Maritime Iberville, where the large cruise ships dock; one may be in port when you pass by.

Continue straight ahead along the promenade to:

6. **Parc des Ecluses** (Locks Park), a popular place to stroll and watch the tour boats along the canal. The first locks on the St. Lawrence River are here, and this is also the starting point for the:

7. **Lachine Canal.** The canal takes its name from the Lachine Rapids, named by explorer Jacques Cartier who got hung up on them just west of the island that would become Montréal. He named them "La Chine" (China), assuming (or perhaps hoping) that China lay on the other side of them.

As early as 1689, the Sulpicians tried to build a canal to avoid the toss-and-tumble Lachine Rapids that prohibited navigation of the St. Lawrence River just upstream. These early efforts failed, and it was not until 1821 to 1825, with the effort of more than 500 Irish workers, that the first Lachine Canal was successfully completed. It was enlarged and lengthened from 1843 to 1849, requiring the muscle power of more than 1,600 workers of Irish origin. The workers lived in barracks near the construction sites, and in 1843 they launched an unsuccessful strike to protest their low pay and poor working conditions.

The canal joined a vast system providing navigation into Upper Canada and the Great Lakes along the 744-mile-long (1,200-kilometer-long) St. Lawrence River, the largest river flowing into the Atlantic in the Northern Hemisphere.

Industries developed along the canal to take advantage of the hydroelectric power so readily available, but the opening of the St. Lawrence Seaway in 1959 tolled the decline of the Lachine Canal, which was closed to navigation in 1970. It found new life in 1978 when it was taken over by Parks Canada, which maintains it as a recreational area with walking and biking paths along its banks. The 7-mile (11-kilometer) cycling path is lit at night and is open from sunrise to midnight; in winter, it handily converts into cross-country ski trails.

REFUELING STOP Enjoy a snack cafeteria-style at **Maison des Ecluses Café** (Locks House Café) in Parc des Ecluses, in the modern structure near the park entry and the lock. The glass facade provides a fine view of tour boats passing by. The café is only open in summer.

Or grab a table at **L'Arrivage,** in the Museum of Archaeology and History at Pointe-à-Callière, and enjoy the view of the Old Port. It's open year-round.

As you begin to make your way through the park, which hugs the canal, keep the canal on your left and rue de la Commune to your right. The canal walk will take at least an hour if you walk briskly; figure on at least 70 minutes at a more leisurely pace.

Soon after you start out, you'll pass a couple of abandoned grain silos before you come to:

8. **Farine Five Roses,** on your left, typical of the flour mills built along the canal. This one is still in operation, but two immense ones were demolished in the 1970s.

Here the road turns, and you'll walk under Highway 10, following the bike path. You are now at Griffintown, and here you will find a Lachine Canal Park map.

The neighborhood known as Griffintown, named after early resident Mary Griffin, expanded greatly during the building of the Lachine Canal and was populated mostly by Irish immigrants who arrived in the mid 1840s. By the turn of the century, Griffintown had 30,000 inhabitants; its sidewalks were wooden, and its streets unpaved.

When the St. Lawrence Seaway opened in 1959, Griffintown took a quick nosedive. The area was zoned for industrial use in 1963, and no one could build or even renovate houses after that. The railway bridges and the Bonaventure Autoroute also did their share to sound the community's death knell.

Study the canal park map. As it indicates, you can continue the walk on either side of the canal. Head in the direction of Lachine.

Take an immediate right at the map and do not cross the bridge. From here, you'll see picnic tables, benches, and a vista of the modern Montréal skyline. Follow the footpath by the water.

When you get to rue du Séminaire and a brick building with blue siding (it's the distribution center for Post Canada), you are almost halfway to the end of the canal walk—unless, of course, you're planning to walk back.

Past this building, there is a view of the 300-foot-high Radio

Canada tower on Mont-Royal (it's three times higher than the cross). When you get to the wooden footbridge, cross it and continue along the path on the other side. You'll see an abandoned factory, designated "Redpath," on the left, as well as a new brick building, "Sodim."

Then you'll arrive at Lock 3 and a waterfall. Cross the bridge (this is rue des Seigneurs) and pick up the path on the lefthand side of the canal. You'll notice that the canal is much wider at this point. You'll see a sign that says LACHINE 10KM. The Atwater Market, which is your destination, is approximately ⅓ mile (½ kilometer) away.

Ahead on the right is a six-story brick complex and a concrete water tower. These are condominiums, and you're almost at the end of the canal walk for our purposes, although the path along the canal actually extends almost 7 miles (11 kilometers) to St-Louis Lake.

The clock tower ahead of you is your goal. Pass by the bridge at rue Charlevoix and continue to the next bridge.

REFUELING STOP There are places to get snacks in the market (the next stop on this tour), but if you've worked up an appetite for a hearty meal, stop right here at rue Charlevoix. **Magnan** (pronounced more or less like MAN-*yah*, though English speakers sometimes rhyme the pronunciation with "canyon"), at rue Charlevoix and rue St-Patrick, is one of Montréal's old stand-bys. The specialty here is steak (year-round) and lobster (in season). Magnan is known for having some of the lowest prices in town, so enjoy the food, the freewheeling ambience, and the value. Downstairs is a little more formal than upstairs.

Follow the canal walk past rue Charlevoix; cross the gently arching aquamarine bridge leading to the:
9. **Atwater Market,** with its easily recognizable tower. The market has been here since 1933. Large and lively, it teems with vendors selling fruit, vegetables, cheese, bread, wine, and flowers; outdoor stalls are covered by a canopy of giant umbrellas. In the summer, fish lovers can catch their own fish in the market's pool. You may be surprised to hear mostly English spoken here, but this is the predominantly English-speaking area of Montréal.

Atwater Market is open daily regular business hours from April to November (to 9pm on Thursday and Friday). In

THE PORT OF MONTREAL

Today the port of Montréal, with piers stretching 16 miles (25 kilometers) between the Cité du Havre and the refineries of Montréal East, is one of the largest ports in the world and the most important inland port in North America. Some 40 shipping companies make Montréal their home; from here they can ship goods inland as far as the Great Lakes along the St. Lawrence River, one of the world's great rivers.

Port activity used to be centered along the quays of what today is known as the Old Port. The port was first established in 1830 to compete with (and later overshadow) the active port at Québec City. In 1853 a direct shipping line was set up between Montréal and Liverpool, England.

The quays of the Old Port were planned by an engineer named John Kennedy in 1877. The piers were set 10 meters above water level to protect them from ice breakup in the spring and to accommodate a new generation of ships.

In 1975, ships began docking downstream at more modern facilities, leaving the Old Port abandoned. For years, Montréalers yearned to have access to the water, but were relegated to traveling to nearby Ile Ste-Hélène or Ile Notre-Dame to get close to it—a pleasant journey, for sure, but frustrating to Montréalers who lived and worked near the water but couldn't get to it.

In the early 1980s, the federal government earmarked $100 million for revitalizing the Old Port (as it did for the port areas of Halifax and Toronto as well). When the city decided to move the commercial part of the port elsewhere, there was talk of building condos by the water, but the idea was quickly squelched. At one point, there was also talk of installing three large fountains at the main entrances to the port but that never happened.

To date, Montréal has invested $65 million of that money to breathe new life into and beautify its Old Port, and the remaining $35 million will most likely go to rejuvenate the wharves.

December, it becomes a veritable Christmas-tree farm. You'll find rest rooms inside the main building.

REFUELING STOP Take a break at **Les Douceurs du Marché,** which means "Market Treats," in the main building at the rue Notre-Dame end of the market (the end opposite from where you arrived). Here you can get a variety of desserts like truffle cake, cheesecake, and fruit torte, and your own plunger-pot of coffee or tea. The place only has four tables seating one or two people each—good luck snagging one—but you can also get coffees and sweets to go.

After exploring the market you have several options. If you're feeling energetic and enjoying the outdoors, you can follow the canal path back the way you came to the Old Port and Old Montréal. If you're tired, you can get the metro at nearby Lionel-Groulx station. If you're still energetic but want to see something new, you can walk along rue Notre-Dame to enjoy the shops that are part of the city's fun antiques district.

I'll lead the way to the antiques stores: Walk to rue Atwater and rue Ste-Emile, and then one more block on rue Atwater to the second set of lights. This is rue Notre-Dame, and you'll turn right onto it. This is the beginning of Montréal's:

10. antiques district, almost 40 shops stretching out along rue Notre-Dame, selling furniture from Québec and Europe. (In 1987, one lucky treasure hunter along this "Antiques Alley" found five small Paleolithic sculptures among the Victorian teacups in a shop called Napoleon Antiques. Known as the Venus figurines, they are believed to predate Christ by 25,000 to 30,000 years.)

Convenient for the browser, most of the shops here are clustered between rue Atwater and rue Vinet, but if you keep walking, you'll find them as far as rue Guy, including one called Ambiance (1874 rue Notre-Dame, at rue des Seigneurs) that doubles as a tearoom and a restaurant. It's open daily for lunch, for Sunday brunch, and for dinner from Wednesday to Sunday.

When you're ready to give your feet a break, you can catch bus no. 35 along rue Notre-Dame; it'll take you to rue Guy, where you can catch the metro.

Olympic Park & the Botanical Garden

Start: Biodome.
Finish: Decorative Arts Museum.
Time: 3 to 4 hours.
Metro: Viau (Biodome exit) to visit the Biodome and Olympic Tower; to go directly to the Botanical Garden or the Decorative Arts Museum, get off at the Pie IX stop.
Best Time: Start out in the morning, so you'll have the whole day to explore. The attractions stay open until 5 or 6pm, later in the summer (except for the Decorative Arts Museum).
Worst Time: Monday or Tuesday, when the Decorative Arts Museum is closed.

For a fun, freewheeling day, head out to Olympic Park, site of the 1976 Olympic Games. Some unique attractions are housed here in recycled Olympic structures, and nearby is the Botanical Garden, second only to Kew Gardens in London for the diversity of its collections.

You'll get a view of the city from the Olympic Tower, an idea of the flora and fauna of the province at the Biodome, and a look at contemporary international design at the Decorative Arts Museum. (Note that in the summer, a free shuttle bus links the metro, Biodome, and Botanical Garden throughout the day.)

Exiting the metro, walk toward and around the flying-saucer–shaped building to its entrance. This is the ecologically oriented:

1. Biodome, which served as the Olympic velodrome in 1976. Both it and the adjacent stadium (and ever-visible Olympic Tower) were designed by the French architect Roger Tailibert.

In the Biodome, which opened in 1992, pathways lead through four ecosystems typical of Québec province. Large, hollow, artificial rocks conceal an elaborate system of pipes for heating and water distribution.

At the entrance to the Biodome, nature films are shown on a globelike screen, and to the left of it, there is a model of the Biodome itself to help you get your bearings. At the center of the complex, the Carrefour de l'Environment (Environmental Cross-roads) provides changing exhibits, talks, and films.

Even if you decide to pass up touring the Biodome, which charges an admission, you can enter the Touristic Hall for free and go downstairs to the Naturalia Exhibit, popular with small children. Rest rooms are downstairs as well.

If you decide to venture into the Biodome, you'll start out in the Tropical Rain Forest, kept at a steamy 22 to 28 degrees Celsius (72 to 82 degrees Fahrenheit) with 75% humidity. Among the inhabitants are turtles, golden lion tamarins, anacondas, sloths, a webbed-footed mammal called a capybara, piranhas, and colorful tropical birds.

In contrast to the rain forest, the next ecosystem, the Laurentian Forest, is cool and refreshing. Here you'll spot some nice-sized brook trout, otters, and beavers, as well as indigenous trees such as maples, birch, aspen, and conifers.

The St. Lawrence ecosystem highlights the changing landscape along one of the world's longest rivers, changing from river to estuary to gulf along the way. A wonderful river wall reveals cod, crabs, and striped bass (I spotted one playful fish rolling over to scratch its back as dogs do); look up to see the bellies and feet of ducks floating on top of the water. You'll also see black ducks, green-winged teals, and night herons hanging out beside small saltwater pools, and a pond inhabited by marine birds—terns, northern gannets, kittiwakes, and storm-petrels—who make their homes in the cliffs above.

The fourth and final ecosystem in the Biodome is the Arctic,

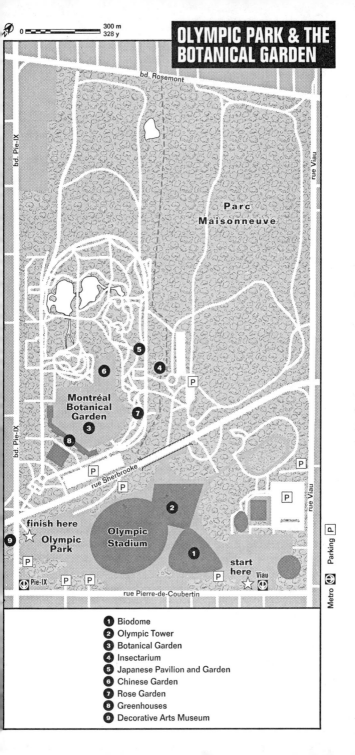

OLYMPIC PARK & THE BOTANICAL GARDEN

0 ____ 300 m
____ 328 y

bd. Rosemont

bd. Pie-IX

rue Viau

Parc
Maisonneuve

Montréal
Botanical
Garden

bd. Pie-IX

rue Sherbrooke

finish here
☆ Olympic
Park

Olympic
Stadium

start
here
☆

Pie-IX

rue Pierre-de-Coubertin

Viau

Metro ⬤   Parking P

1 Biodome
2 Olympic Tower
3 Botanical Garden
4 Insectarium
5 Japanese Pavilion and Garden
6 Chinese Garden
7 Rose Garden
8 Greenhouses
9 Decorative Arts Museum

home to puffins and penguins. You'll see Arctic penguins dive underwater (in the wild, these birds swim at average speeds of 15 miles, or 24 kilometers, an hour) and hear them in conversation with their young.

REFUELING STOP   The **cafeteria** in the Biodome is well-stocked and inexpensive, with everything from yogurt, salads, and muffins to pizza and hot meals. There's also a small **snack bar** in the Olympic Tower, which is next on the walking tour; the surroundings there are more pleasant than in the Biodome's cafeteria, but the menu is more limited (mainly sandwiches and burgers).

Exit the Biodome, cross the courtyard, and follow the signs to the:

2. **Olympic Tower** (Tour). The 626-foot, 183,000-ton inclined tower (the tallest in the world) is a Montréal landmark, visible from many places in the city. It is an integral part of Olympic Park and is now part of a center for swimming and sports events.

If you decide to ride to the top of it, first buy your ticket at the booths just inside the entrance, then follow the signs to the "Funiculaire," which runs every 10 to 15 minutes. On the ride up (down, too), you'll notice a pyramid-like building; it's actually two apartment buildings constructed in 1976 to serve as the Olympic Village. Besides 950 apartments, the complex has two floors of offices, a medical clinic, and a physical fitness center. Beyond it lie the Laurentian Mountains. The Botanical Garden is to your left and the city is directly behind you (you'll see it from the observation deck).

From the observation deck at the top, you can look down on the stadium, which can accommodate up to 80,000 people for Expos baseball games, rock concerts, and other events. The 65-ton retractable Kevlar roof is suspended by 125 tons of steel cables, and the inclined tower is essential to its operation. It takes 45 minutes to raise or lower the roof, as 45 computer-controlled winches operate it slowly up or down. Because of its sophisticated technology, the stadium has been called "the most costly on the planet"—as Québec taxpayers still point out.

As you gaze out at the city from here, can you spot La Ronde, the city's amusement park? (The park behind La Ronde, Parc Ste-Hélène, is one of the city's prettiest.) The casino on Ile Notre-Dame? And St-Joseph's Oratory? Be sure to take a good look at the layout of the Botanical Garden—its centerpiece is a Chinese Garden—since it'll be your next destination.

Exit the Olympic Tower through the glass doors when you get off the funicular; outside, take the stairs to your left. Go up two flights of steps, follow the path, cross rue Sherbrooke at the traffic light, and head into the:

3. **Botanical Garden,** founded in 1931 by Brother Marie-Victorin (1885–1944) of the Ecoles Chretiennes (Christian Schools). The first phase of work on the 180-acre garden took place from 1936 to 1938; today there are more than 26,000 kinds of plants in 30 specialized gardens and 10 greenhouses. Roses bloom from mid-June to the first frost, May is the month for lilacs, and June for the flowering hawthorn trees. Additionally, more than 130 species of birds spend at least part of the year here.

When you enter the garden, follow the black paved path, keeping the stone building with the brown roof to your left. Parc Maisonneuve, popular for jogging, cycling, and cross-country skiing and site of a nine-hole golf course, will be to your right.

Walk to the circular drive, and to the back entrance of the Botanical Garden. Here you pay your admission, which includes the gardens, greenhouses, and Insectarium (see below). Inside the garden, you'll find yourself almost at the front door of the:

4. **Insectarium,** an airy, two-level complex devoted to insects from the ridiculous to the sublime. The super black-and-gold spider, *argiope aurantia,* at the entrance let's you know what's in store (though what you see will be on a smaller scale).

Get ready to gaze at mounted scorpions, scarabs, maggots, locusts, beetles (including one named Goliath), tarantulas, and

THE ENDANGERED SPECIES OF THE ST. LAWRENCE

There are only an estimated 500 beluga whales in the St. Lawrence River today, compared to 5,000 in 1885. To protect those remaining, the Saguenay Marine Park was established to preserve their natural environment. Other endangered species in the St. Lawrence include humpback whales, the Atlantic sturgeon, and the striped bass. All have been put at risk due to habitat destruction, pollution, and overharvesting.

giraffe weevils—some 3,000 in all, and the collections of two avid entomologists, Georges Brossad (who envisioned Insectarium) and Father Firmia Liberté. There are also live exhibits featuring crickets, cockroaches, and praying mantises.

From the Insectarium, follow the brick walkway around the side of the building; take the path on the left, cross the road, and go through the Aquatic Garden, with its welcoming fountains, and through an area filled with roses (you'll visit the park's major Rose Garden later). Follow any of the paths to the right. When you see the brown building, you'll know you have arrived at the:

5. Japanese Pavilion and Garden, which opened in 1988. The building, in Sukiya design, is typical of traditional Japanese homes. Inside there is an exhibit hall, an art gallery, library, tea room, and a contemplative Zen garden. Three Japanese women serve tea and cakes (for a fee) in the tea garden May through August several times during the afternoon.

In the Nomura exhibition space, you'll see traditional screens, samurai outfits, and geisha hairstyles and robes. Changing exhibits are mounted in the Daishowa Gallery, at the back of the pavilion.

Outside is a 6-acre (2.5-hectare) Japanese garden of pure harmony where peonies, rhododendrons, irises, crab-apple trees, and perennials flourish. Walk to the waterfall at the far end of it and soak up this tranquility of sight and sound. In summer, 30 miraculous specimens of 25- to 350-year-old bonsai trees await you in their special garden.

Exiting the Japanese Pavilion, take the path to the right. When it forks, go left, and proceed through the roses again, past a flagstone path, and on to a second walkway. It will be on your right, with a large stone structure beside it marking the way to the main entrance of the:

6. Chinese Garden. This 6-acre (2.5-hectare) complex has seven classical pavilions with clay-tile roofs curving up to meet the sky and graceful Ming-epoch gardens. All the pavilions were made in Shanghai, disassembled, brought to Montréal, and reassembled by Chinese craftspeople in 1991. No nails were used in the construction. The garden, the largest of its kind outside of Asia, is dedicated to dreams and friendship.

Walk through the low white building to get to the garden's largest pavilion, the Friendship Hall, or cultural center, a gift from the city of Shanghai. The terrace at the back of it overlooks the Lake of Dreams, and the view from here is known as "Dawn on Dream Lake."

The lake, the centerpiece of the garden, measures 197 by 131 feet (60 by 40 meters) and all the pavilions are situated around it.

To explore them, follow the circular path around the lake, starting to your right and walking in a counterclockwise direction.

At the pavilion called the Tower of the Condensing Clouds, across the lake from the Friendship Hall, you'll get a beautiful view of the garden with the Olympic Tower behind it (talk about yin and yang). In summer, you can visit the Penjing Garden, with its display of dwarf trees. (The Chinese art of penjing, which dates from 265 to 420 AD, preceded the Japanese art of bonsai by about 250 years. Both are amply represented in Montréal's Botanical Garden.)

After you've walked around the lake, go back through the large Friendship Hall and go out the same way you came in, past the stone sculpture. From here, turn right and walk toward the Olympic Tower, an easy landmark.

Follow the "Serres" (greenhouses) signs via a path that takes you through the:

7. Rose Garden, filled with 7,000 rosebushes of every conceivable shape and color. Look for such varieties as the Hybrid Tea, Old Tea, Floribunda, and Grandiflora, and miniature and newer hybrids specially cultivated to adapt to the Québec climate. They sweeten the air every year from June through October.

At the end of this walk, follow the path beside the black fence to your left, toward the low, brown brick building in art deco style. This is the garden's administration building and research institute. When you get closer to it, take a moment to notice the four bas-reliefs in the facade, created by Henri Hébert. They depict Amerindian scenes: a woman crushing corn, two men in a birch-bark canoe, a man collecting sap from a maple tree, and a moose surrounded by water lilies.

Turn right and walk to the building with the glass doors, which lead to the:

8. greenhouses (serres). They are on both sides of the entrance. Start with the ones on the right to see the orchids, then return to the entry and cross over to the greenhouses on the left to visit the begonias, cacti, and the garden's amazing collection of bonsai.

When you exit the greenhouses, turn right and walk down to the road. In the summer you can take a small train, called the Balade du Jardin, through the 180-acre (73–hectare) garden. It's more than worth the small charge.

After your train ride, take the main exit beyond the large fountain directly in front of the administration building. You'll pass a statue of Brother Marie-Victorin, created by Sylvia Daoust in 1954.

Directly across boulevard Pie IX is the:

BROTHER MARIE-VICTORIN

A self-taught botanist, professor, and scientific researcher and reformer, Brother Marie-Victorin (born Conrad Kirouac) of the Ecoles Chretiennes (Christian Schools) founded the Montréal Botanical Garden and the Botanical Institute at the University of Montréal. In 1935, he received the Prix Courcy from the Academy of Sciences of Paris for his body of work and his book *La Flore Laurentienne*.

The garden Marie-Victorin founded is today bested only by Kew Gardens in London for the size and diversity of its collection.

9. **Decorative Arts Museum,** also known as the Château Dufresne, which you enter from the back through the gates. (You might also want to walk around to the front to see the symmetrical, colonnaded facade.) The building, one of the first in this area to be made of reinforced concrete, is faced with Indiana limestone and has an interior filled with Italian marble and African mahogany.

The house was the private home of two brothers, Oscar and Marius Dufresne, and their families; a common wall separated the house into two dwellings. Marius, an engineer (his brother was an industrialist), designed the house in collaboration with the French architect Jules Renard. It was built between 1916 and 1918 at a cost of $1 million. The Dufresnes filled the house with silver, porcelain, paintings, sculpture, furniture, and textiles of the period.

At the top of the stairs on the second floor, to your left, are 12 panels, painted on canvas between 1920 and 1935 and glued to the wall. Each canvas represents one of the 12 months of the year. The work was done by the Italian artist Guido Nincheri, who lived in Canada; Nincheri also created the stained glass in the house. There is a large ballroom with unique windows on the second floor. When you visit the Salon, give my regards to the nymphs on the ceilings and walls.

On the third floor, be sure to see the colorful room divider by the Italian designer Ettore Sottsass, and the chair and ottoman by Gaetano Pesce. Both artists are Italian and both have pieces exhibited at the Canadian Centre for Architecture. This exhibit space includes wonderful and whimsical chairs and lamps by Japanese, American, Italian, Dutch, and French designers.

The ground floor features changing exhibits; a café; and a shop selling books, jewelry, and household and kitchen items.

REFUELING STOP The pleasant **café** in the Decorative Arts Museum serves light fare that includes soup, salad, and dessert, as well as beer and wine.

Exit the house and turn right. Walk down the hill to the Pie IX metro stop.

Mont-Royal

Start: Park entrance at rue Peel and avenue des Pins.
Finish: The cross on top of the mountain.
Time: 2 hours, allowing for some dawdling. If you're pressed for time, you can get to the lookout in a little more than half an hour and back down the mountain in 15 minutes.
Metro: McGill College.
Best Time: Mornings in spring, summer, and autumn.
Worst Time: Winter, when snow and slush make a sleigh ride to the top of the mountain much more enticing than a walk.

Not many cities have a mountain at their core, but Montréal does; in fact, the city is named for it. The beloved bump on the landscape is simply called "the mountain" by Montréalers, who adore it—with obvious good reason. Many Montréalers have met on the mountain, courted and fallen in love there, and brought their children back to develop their own relationship with it.

Mont-Royal Park, which encompasses the mountain—from whose top you can see the city, the island, and the St. Lawrence River—is a 494-acre (200-hectare) retreat, half of which has been left as natural forest. It was created in 1876 by the American landscape architect Frederick Law Olmsted, the designer of New York City's Central Park and other parks in Philadelphia, Boston, and Chicago.

Olmsted, who believed that nature should be left as unfettered as possible, proposed a system of roads and paths suited to the topography and the landscape. The road you'll be walking on, which has been widened since Olmsted oversaw its creation, is the only part of his plan that was ever realized.

Olmsted encouraged developers to keep in mind the diminutive size of the mountain and not dwarf it with overdevelopment. That didn't stop them, but thankfully most of their embellishments have been done away with over time. He also warned against providing easy access to the mountain, but this suggestion was overridden more than once. From about 1890 to 1918, a funicular operated up and down the mountain from rue Duluth. The charge was 5¢ up and 3¢ down. It was torn down in 1920. A streetcar operated from 1924 to 1957, and today bus 11 follows the old streetcar route.

In 1912, the construction of a tunnel was begun on either side of the mountain; the construction crews met in December 1913, with an error of less than 3 centimeters (1 inch) in alignment and only ½ centimeter (⅕ inch) in height.

Over the years the mountain has been put to good use by Montréalers, who once picnicked in the Notre-Dame-des-Neiges Cemetery (which you'll visit on this tour), hunted here into the 19th century, went horseback riding in the early 1900s, and even played golf at a club on the southeast side of the mountain from 1882 to the turn of the century.

Today (as always, really) the most enjoyable way to explore Mont-Royal and get into Mont-Royal Park is simply to walk into and up it. Joggers, cyclists, lovers, and folks in search of a little peace head here in warm weather. In winter, cross-country skiers follow the miles of paths within the park, and snowshoers tramp and crunch along trails laid out especially for them.

The park is open from 6am to midnight daily. The snack bars at the lookout and Beaver Lake are generally open daily from 9am to 5pm.

Start this tour at the corner of rue Peel and avenue des Pins; you'll be at the unassuming:

1. **Downtown park entrance,** where a handy map can help you get your bearings. From here, you can ascend the mountain in several ways: Hearty souls may choose the quickest and most strenuous approach—scaling the steep slope directly to the lookout at the top; those who prefer to take their time and gain

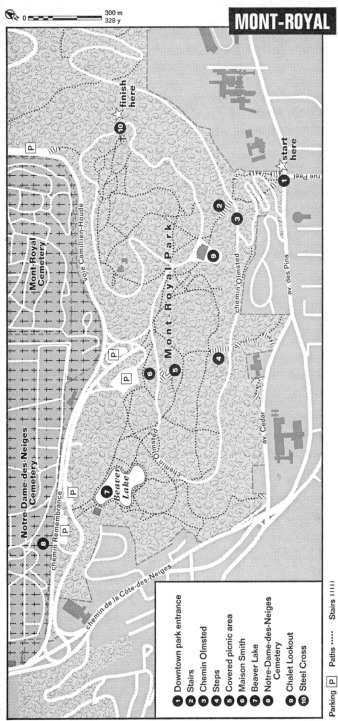

MONT-ROYAL

0 | 300 m / 328 y

★ start here
★ finish here

rue Peel
av. des Pins
chemin Olmsted
av. Cedar
Voie Camillien-Houde
chemin Remembrance
chemin de la Côte-des-Neiges
chemin Olmsted

Mont-Royal Park

Mont-Royal Cemetery

Notre-Dame-des-Neiges Cemetery

Beaver Lake

1 Downtown park entrance
2 Stairs
3 Chemin Olmsted
4 Steps
5 Covered picnic area
6 Maison Smith
7 Beaver Lake
8 Notre-Dame-des-Neiges Cemetery
9 Chalet Lookout
10 Steel Cross

Parking P   Paths ·····   Stairs |||||

6464

altitude slowly may opt for one mild set of stairs followed by a sinuous switchback bridle path (turn left onto it) leading to the top. I fall somewhere in between these two extremes, and I'll share my approach to the mountain with you, while pointing out the other alternatives as you come to them.

I start out, as most people do, by taking the gravel path to the right as you face the map of the park. It has intervals of four steps, and parallels the wall that separates the park from the outside world. When the path dead-ends, turn left (away from some steep steps you'll see beside a small lookout).

If you've decided to take the athletic route, take the next:

2. **stairs** that you come to on the right. There are more than 250 steps in all, and the last 100 go straight up. I prefer to come down them rather than huff and puff my way up them. If you're of the same mind, stick with me on the wide:

3. **chemin Olmsted** (Olmsted Road), named for the park's designer and actually the only part of his design that became a reality. If you stay on this road, which is definitely a slow road, you'll bypass a few of this tour's stops and get to the next stop (number 6) in about 45 minutes.

Frederick Law Olmsted designed the road at such a gradual grade not only for pedestrians, but particularly for horse-drawn carriages (calèches): Horses could pull their load up the hill at a steady pace, and on the way down would not be pushed by the weight of that same load.

Chemin Olmsted is closed to automobiles and open to walkers, joggers, and squirrels, all of which you're bound to meet along the way. Early on, it passes some beautiful stone houses off Redpath Circle, to your left.

You'll see a couple of paths leading up the mountain to the right. They'll get you to your destination more quickly but aren't as strenuous as the steps you've recently bypassed. So if you find the slow road just a little too slow, take the:

4. **steps** leading to an old pump station, to your right. From here continue in an uphill direction until you come to a:

5. **covered picnic area,** an open-air stone-and-wood structure with a copper roof. Walk around behind the shelter and take the stairway behind it down the hill, which will deposit you back on chemin Olmsted (minus a couple of big loops you've edited out of your walk). You're now standing at the back of the:

6. **Maison Smith** (Smith House), which was built in 1858 and has been used as a park rangers station and park police headquarters. From 1983 to 1992 it served as a small nature museum, however it was not open to the public at this writing. There's a parking lot

beside the house, and nearby you'll see the 300-foot-high Radio Canada Tower.

From the house, walk through the field of sculptures (away from the parking lot and the radio tower) to arrive at:

7. Beaver Lake (Lac des Castors). In summer, it is surrounded by sunbathers and picnickers and filled with boaters, and in the cold winter months before the snow sets in it becomes an ice skater's paradise. Once the pond is covered with snow, the small ski tow starts operation, tugging novice skiers up the gentle slope for another practice run down and across the pond's face.

There is a small concession stand here, but if you plan to have something to eat or drink on the mountain, choose the concession at the chalet at the nearby lookout rather than the pavilion at the lake. Both the chalet and the pavilion have rest rooms and telephones.

Walk across the road, called chemin de la Remembrance (Remembrance Road), behind the pavilion, to enter:

8. Notre-Dame-des-Neiges Cemetery, the city's enormous and beautiful Catholic cemetery. (If you wanted to make a day of exploring cemeteries you could go from here to the adjacent Protestant Cemetery, and then behind it, to the small Jewish, Spanish, and Portuguese cemetery, but it would be a challenging and time-consuming walk.) Notre-Dame-des-Neiges Cemetery reveals some of the ethnic mix in Montréal. You'll see headstones, some with likenesses in photos or tiles, for Montréalers with surnames as diverse as Zagorska, Skwyrska, De Ciccio, Sen, Lavoie, Barrett, O'Neill, Hammerschmid, Fernandez, Muller, Giordano, Haddad, and Boudreault.

Explore this part of the cemetery, then retrace your steps to chemin Olmsted, pass the Smith House again, and continue along the road for a few minutes until you come to a water fountain embedded in a granite slab. Take the narrow, winding path below it through the trees. Along the way look for a tree trunk carved by artist Jacques Morin in 1986; part of the inscription explains a little of what you see—an "old, sick tree, sculpted and transformed, neither male nor female. . . ."

The path leads to the:

9. Chalet Lookout. The chalet was constructed in 1931 and 1932, at a cost of $230,000 Canadian, and has been used over the years for receptions and concerts. Inside the chalet, note the 17 paintings hanging just below the ceiling, starting to the right of the door that leads into the snack bar; they tell the story of the history of the region as well as the French explorations in North America.

The exhibit inside is provided by the Environmental Education Center on Mont-Royal. The front terrace, a magnet for Montréalers of all ages, provides a panoramic view of the city and the river. In winter, there's a warming room for skiers here.

REFUELING STOP   At the **concession stand** in the chalet, you can get sandwiches, muffins, apples, ice cream, milk, juice, tea, and coffee. Heed the signs that ask you to refrain from feeding the squirrels that you will see begging so politely and convincingly. These cute scavengers can find plenty to eat on the mountain, but they're not above snatching food right out of people's hands.

As you face the chalet from the terrace, you'll see a path off to the right. Follow it for about eight minutes to a giant:

10. steel cross, which you've no doubt seen more than once from a distance if you've been in Montréal any length of time; it's a definitive part of the Montréal skyline. Tradition has it that Maisonneuve erected a wooden cross here in 1642. The modern incarnation, erected in 1924, is rigged for illumination at night, making it visible from all over the city.

Beside the cross is a green plaque marking the spot where a time capsule was placed in August of 1992, during Montréal's 350th birthday celebration. Some 12,000 children ages 6 to 12 filled the capsule with messages and drawings depicting their visions for the city in the year 2,142—when Montréal will be 500 years old, and when the capsule will be opened.

To return to downtown Montréal, you can retrace your steps to the chalet terrace. On the left, just before you get to the terrace, you'll see a path. It leads to the 250 or so steps that will take you back down to where you began this tour, at the entrance to the park. You can also catch bus no. 11 at Beaver Lake, hop off at chemin de la Remembrance and Côte-des-Neiges, and pick up bus no. 165, which will deposit you at the Guy metro station.

REFUELING STOP   If you've ended your tour at the park entrance again, you're probably ready for some rest and refreshment. Walk down the hill on rue Peel to rue Sherbrooke, and walk to the Alcan Building, at rue Stanley; you can enter the building from either rue Sherbrooke or rue Stanley. From Sherbrooke, walk to the back of the building's lobby to **La Tulipe Noire** pâtisserie for dessert and coffee or a sandwich. If it's a nice day, be sure and sit outside—the terrace is the special draw here.

WALKING TOUR 5

Downtown Montréal

Start: Dorchester Square.
Finish: McCord Museum of Canadian History.
Time: 1½ hours, not including museum stops.
Metro: Bonaventure or Peel.
Best Time: Weekday mornings or after 2pm, when the streets hum with big-city vibrancy but aren't too crowded.
Worst Time: Noon to 2pm weekdays, when the streets, stores, and restaurants are crowded with businessfolk on the loose; and weekends, when people have deserted the downtown area for their country places. Also, if you want to tour the Musée des Beaux-Arts and the McCord, remember that both are closed on Mondays.

Downtown Montréal is a vital place, and it has been since the early 1960s. It contains not only the commercial heart of the city, but also restaurants, modern shopping complexes, historical churches and buildings, and several highly regarded museums. And, like the rest of the city, it's very walkable.

To see for yourself, take the metro to the Bonaventure stop (exit at the Queen Elizabeth Hotel, walk west on boulevard René-Lévesque 1 block to Metcalfe, turn right and walk 1 block) or the Peel stop (walk 1 block south on Peel, crossing Ste-Catherine). You'll be in the center of the downtown shopping and business district at:

1. Dorchester Square, known as Dominion Square until 1987. It used to be the scene of Montréal's winter carnival and the setting for an enormous ice palace built for the festivities (since 1982 the Fête des Neiges has been held at the Old Port, Ile Ste-Hélène, and Ile Notre-Dame). Notable on the square today is the Sun Life Building, on rue Metcalfe and boulevard René-Lévesque. It was constructed, in three stages, from 1914 to 1931, and for many years it faced the old Windsor Hotel (1878) across the square. Inspired by New York's Waldorf Astoria, the Windsor was once one of the largest hotels in North America. Today the Banque du Commerce, formerly the Canadian Imperial Bank of Commerce, built from 1959 to 1962, rises on the spot where the hotel once stood.

Along the square, a row of calèches (horse-drawn carriages) waits patiently. In winter the calèche drivers replace their carriages with horse-drawn sleighs and give rides to the top of Mont-Royal.

Dorchester Square was sliced in two in the mid-1950s when boulevard René-Lévesque (then known as boulevard Dorchester) was widened; the southern part of the square is now known as place du Canada. In it stands a statue of Sir John A. MacDonald, the first prime minister of Canada. It was created in 1894 by English sculptor George Wade.

On the northern side of Dorchester Square is the tourist information office:

2. Infotouriste. If you need a map or other information, now's your chance to get it. At Infotouriste you can also buy guidebooks and coffee-table tomes about the city, make hotel or car-rental bookings, and change money at a currency-exchange window.

From the southern end of Dorchester Square, walk east along:

3. boulevard René-Lévesque. Formerly Dorchester Boulevard, this street was renamed in 1987 following the death of the Parti Québécois leader who had led the movement in favor of Québec independence and the use of the French language. Boulevard René-Lévesque is the city's broadest downtown thoroughfare, and the one with the fastest traffic, so be careful when you cross it.

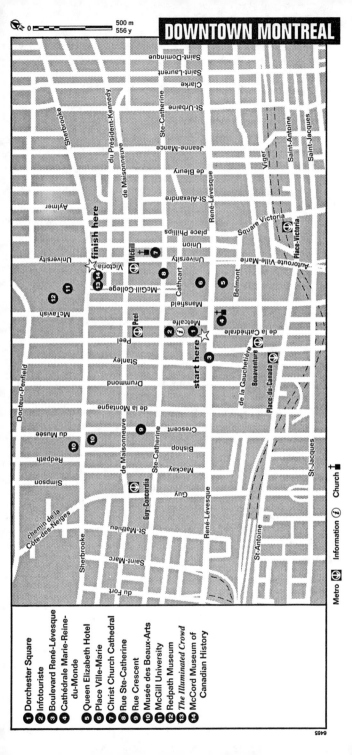

DOWNTOWN MONTREAL

0 ————— 500 m
————— 556 y

Metro 🔵 Information ⓘ Church †

1 Dorchester Square
2 Infotouriste
3 Boulevard René-Lévesque
4 Cathédrale Marie-Reine-du-Monde
5 Queen Elizabeth Hotel
6 Place Ville-Marie
7 Christ Church Cathedral
8 Rue Ste-Catherine
9 Rue Crescent
10 Musée des Beaux-Arts
11 McGill University
12 Redpath Museum
13 *The Illuminated Crowd*
14 McCord Museum of Canadian History

start here

finish here

6465

On the right, just past rue de la Cathédrale, is a faithful copy of Saint Peter's Basilica in Rome, built on a smaller scale and named:

4. **Cathédrale Marie-Reine-du-Monde** (Cathedral of Mary, Queen of the World), built between 1875 and 1894 and the headquarters for Montréal's Roman Catholic bishop. The statue in front of the cathedral is of Bishop Ignace Bourget (1799–1885); it was sculpted in 1903 by Louis-Philippe Hébert, creator of the well-known statue of Maisonneuve in place d'Armes.

Across rue Mansfield from the cathedral is the:

5. **Queen Elizabeth Hotel,** built in 1958, the year before Queen Elizabeth II and U.S. president Dwight D. Eisenhower officially opened the St. Lawrence Seaway. The hotel, which was renovated in the early 1990s, has hosted numerous celebrities, among them Nat King Cole, Carol Channing, and John Lennon and Yoko Ono.

The hotel is a central transportation point for tourists; from here you can board a sightseeing bus, get a train at Windsor Station, or catch the bus to Dorval or Mirabel Airport.

Across boulevard Réne-Lévesque from the Queen Elizabeth is:

6. **place Ville-Marie.** Known simply as "PVM" to Montréalers, the square was the keystone of downtown's early urban redevelopment efforts. The cross-shaped skyscraper on the square is the Royal Bank of Canada building, designed by I. M. Pei. Both the shape of this building and the square's name recall Cartier's cross, planted to claim the island for France, and Maisonneuve's first little settlement, named Ville-Marie.

The sleek and streamlined building was completed in 1962, and the three other buildings in the complex were built within the next four years. The fountain on the plaza is called *Feminine Landscape* (1972) and was executed by Toronto artist Gerald Gladstone.

From place Ville-Marie, turn left onto rue University and walk the 2 blocks to rue Ste-Catherine for a look at:

7. **Christ Church Cathedral** (built 1856 to 1859), a fine Gothic building and the seat of the Anglican bishop of Montréal. The cathedral's 127-foot aluminum-covered steel steeple replaced a heavier stone one that proved too heavy. The church spire is visible through the 47-foot-high lobby of the skyscraper place de la Cathedral, and the Cloister Garden is modeled on a medieval European cloister. The cathedral donated the land on which the place de la Cathédrale and the shopping complex underneath it,

Promenades de la Cathédrale, are built, and in the year 2,063 ownership of the skyscraper and the underground complex will revert to it. In the meantime, the new construction has shored up the structurally sagging cathedral.

Turn left on:

8. rue Ste-Catherine, undeniably a shopper's street, and head northwest, through the center of Montréal's shopping and entertainment district. Most of the giant department stores are here, including La Baie (or The Bay, short for Hudson's Bay Company, successor to the famous fur-trapping firm), Eaton, and Ogilvy (see "Walking Tour 7—A Shopper's Walk," for more information). Movie houses, restaurants, and shops line rue Ste-Catherine all the way—about 8 blocks—to the popular (particularly with tourists) dining and shopping area centered around:

9. rue Crescent. This area that now bustles with nightlife was once a run-down slum area slated for demolition. Luckily, individual buyers with good aesthetic sense saw the possibilities of the delightful old houses here and brought them back to life through renovation. If you like rue Crescent, go around the corner to rue Bishop, a similar type of street that has a comedy club (Comedy Works at no. 1238) to rival the one on rue Crescent (Comedy Nest at no. 1459).

REFUELING STOP For a memorable Indian meal, experience **Bukhara,** at 2100 rue Crescent. The restaurant is quiet, sleek, and serene—modern yet tempered with the warmth of brick and wood. By all means, try the dahl, made here from a secret recipe with a tomato base. The waiters encourage you to eat with your hands and offer aprons to catch any spills (if you protest, cutlery is forthcoming), and they provide finger bowls before and after the meal. Portions—even the salads—are large.

Head up rue Crescent, past rue Maisonneuve, to the corner of rues Crescent and Sherbrooke. On both sides of rue Sherbrooke is the:

10. Musée des Beaux-Arts (Museum of Fine Arts), Canada's oldest and Montréal's finest museum, with an extensive collection of more than 25,000 items. The original Greek Revival building (1912) on the north side of Sherbrooke, known as the Benaiah Gibb Pavilion, is devoted to art of the Americas:

TOUR DE L'ILE

Early in June each year, usually the first Sunday of the month, the Tour de l'Ile, a 40-mile (65-kilometer) tour of the city takes place, and the downtown streets are closed to traffic for the event. Some 45,000 participants take part, and 100,000 people turn out to cheer them on. But this is not a race—it's more a celebration of a city that is unusually biker-friendly, with 149 miles (240 kilometers) of bike paths to its credit.

The average speed in the Tour de l'Ile varies between 7 and 19 miles (12 and 30 kilometers) per hour, though the serious cyclists (about 1,300 of them) start out ahead of the group and average 22 miles (35 kilometers) per hour. There are five rest stations along the way. There's even a "sag wagon" to take those who poop out before the end to the finish line to join the others. The main purpose of the event is to have fun and explore the island of Montréal, from downtown to the less-well-known outlying areas.

The Tour de l'Ile has been a Montréal tradition since 1985. The route varies from year to year, but it usually kicks off and ends near the base of Mont-Royal in downtown. The *Guinness Book of World Records* recognizes it as the largest gathering of cyclists in the world.

Canadian art before 1960, Meso-American art, Inuit art, and Amerindian art.

An ultramodern annex, the Jean-Noel Desmarais Pavilion, is on the south side of Sherbrooke. Opened in late 1991, it is devoted to contemporary international art and Canadian art after 1960, and to European paintings, sculpture, and decorative arts from the Middle Ages to the 19th century. This new annex more than doubled the museum's exhibit space, with galleries on six levels (four above ground and two below); its surprisingly placed windows and angles reveal the city when you least suspect it. The architect, Boston-based Moshe Safdie, incorporated into his design the facade of a 1902 apartment building that the citizens did not want torn down.

The two pavilions are connected by an underground tunnel that also serves as a large gallery devoted to the art of ancient cultures.

Texts in the museum are in French and English, and the special exhibits in both pavilions are dependably noteworthy.

Leaving the museum, walk 6 blocks east on rue Sherbrooke; soon you'll come to the campus of:

11. McGill University, one of Canada's most prestigious institutions of higher learning. In 1811, a fur trader and entrepreneur named James McGill bequeathed £10,000 and 46 acres of farmland for the establishment of a college. All he asked was that the school be named after him. At that time rue Sherbrooke was only a dirt road, far from the center of town. When the first building, the Arts Building, opened, only three students applied for entrance. The front lawn was a pasture.

The university actually started as a medical school by incorporating itself with an existing school, the Montréal Medical Institution (originally located at place d'Armes). Today McGill remains outstanding in medicine and the sciences.

Feel free to wander around the beautiful campus, with its green lawns mounting the slopes of Mont-Royal. On the campus is the:

12. Redpath Museum, at 859 rue Sherbrooke ouest. The building dates from 1882, and the main draw here is the Egyptian antiquities collection, the second largest collection of its kind in Canada.

Opposite the university and just half a block south of rue Sherbrooke on broad, striking rue McGill College is an unusual butter-colored sculpture called:

13. *The Illuminated Crowd,* by Toronto artist Raymond Mason. Take the time to ponder it from every vantage point; the facial expressions of crowd members change as you move from front to back, running the gamut of human emotions.

Return to rue Sherbrooke and continue to make your way east 1 block to the:

14. McCord Museum of Canadian History (690 rue Sherbrooke ouest), first opened in 1921 and impressively renovated and expanded in 1992. The private museum's changing exhibits showcase the eclectic (sometimes eccentric) 80,000-artifact collection of museum founder David Ross McCord (1844–1930), a merchant whose family immigrated to Québec from Northern Ireland in 1760.

Furniture, clothing, china, silver, paintings, photographs, and folk art reveal middle and upper class, mostly English-speaking European-immigrant city life, as well as rural life, mostly from the 18th through 20th centuries. Amerindians are represented by exhibits of MicMac clothing, jewelry, and beautiful beadwork purses, pouches, sashes, and moccasins. A weathered totem pole from British Columbia spans the museum's three floors. Outside of the museum stands the imposing Inuit sculpture, *Inukskuk,* created with more than 300 stones. (Exhibit texts are in English and French.)

REFUELING STOP   There's a tearoom on the ground floor of the McCord Museum which you can visit even if you don't tour the museum. Have a snack and decide what's next on your Montréal itinerary.

A Modern Architecture Tour

Start: World Trade Centre.
Finish: The Laurentian Bank Building, or the Canadian Centre for Architecture.
Time: 2 hours (3½ if you visit the Canadian Centre for Architecture).
Metro: Place Victoria.
Best Time: During the day, when the buildings can be seen to their best advantage.
Worst Time: If you plan to visit the Canadian Centre for Architecture at the conclusion of this walk, be aware that it is closed to the public on Monday and Tuesday.

The Montréal skyline is colorful, varied, and engaging. And when you come close to the skyscrapers—none of which, by city ordinance, can be higher than Mont-Royal—they remain compelling. Urban planners and architects have been careful to integrate the old (and there's still plenty of it in the downtown area) and the new, with some creative twists along the way. Montréal may be over 350 years old, but it still manages to come off as a thoroughly, undeniably, excitingly modern city.

You'll start this tour in the old business center, in Old Montréal, and make your way from there to the modern downtown core of buildings. When you get off the metro at place Victoria, walk to the underground rotunda and test out its echo-chamber effect. Take the Centro de Commerce Mondial exit, a long curving brick walkway which leads you into the atrium of the:

1. **World Trade Centre** (Centre de Commerce Mondial), opened in 1992. When this enormous complex rose on the Montréal skyline—right at the junction of Old Montréal and the modern downtown—it kept the significant buildings on the block intact and added to them. The 26-floor, 359-room Hotel Inter-Continental is a good example of the way the Centre mixes old and new architecture: The hotel incorporates an older, existing structure with a new, modern tower.

Only the first three floors in the World Trade Centre are connected by escalators and skywalks (the offices on higher floors are accessible by elevator only and are private). The 600-foot pedestrian walkway you see beneath the soaring atrium follows the line where the old fortification wall around Ville-Marie once stood (on maps it is marked Fortification Lane). Note the two, quite different fountains in the atrium. One represents Amphitrite, the wife of Poseidon, god of the seas. This early-18th-century fountain was purchased in Paris by Paul Desmarais, chairman of the Power Corporation, and given to the city of Montréal. Adjacent to the semi-reclining Amphitrite is a 50-by-30-foot flat black marble slab covered with a sheet of water. This fountain was actually designed as a reflecting pool to mirror the surrounding architecture.

The contemporary gray-stone Power Corporation Building faces the traditional fountain; it, along with the Canada Steamship Lines Companies, was located here before the World Trade Centre was built, as were the Bank of Nova Scotia Building on the southwest side and the Italian Renaissance Nesbitt Thomson Building at the southeast end.

The north and south sections of the complex, which contain shops, restaurants, and offices, are connected by skywalks. There is also an indoor parking space for 600 cars.

The center incorporates 11 heritage buildings in a 4-acre site opposite the Montréal Stock Exchange, notable among them the Nordheimer Building (1888). To see its striking pink-granite facade, and the way it has been integrated into the complex, walk

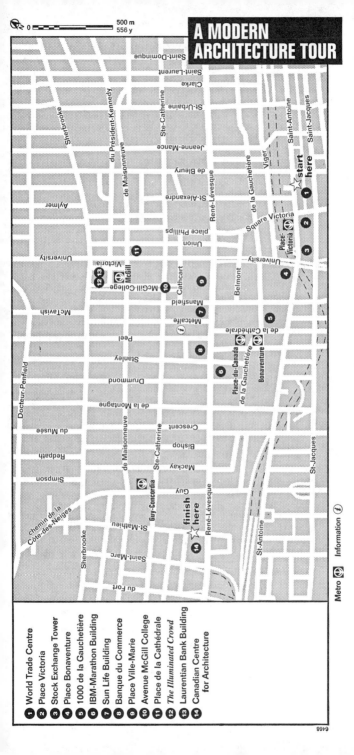

A MODERN ARCHITECTURE TOUR

500 m
556 y

1 World Trade Centre
2 Place Victoria
3 Stock Exchange Tower
4 Place Bonaventure
5 1000 de la Gauchetière
6 IBM-Marathon Building
7 Sun Life Building
8 Banque du Commerce
9 Place Ville-Marie
10 Avenue McGill College
11 Place de la Cathédrale
12 *The Illuminated Crowd*
13 Laurentian Bank Building
14 Canadian Centre for Architecture

Metro Ⓜ   Information ⓘ

start here 1

finish here 14

6466

to the far end of the building to the St-Pierre (or back) entrance. Exit here and turn right to get to rue St-Jacques, known as the city's banking street; cross the street, and turn right again to admire the World Trade Centre and the incorporated facade of the Nordheimer Building.

The Nordheimer Building once housed a piano showroom, offices, and a concert hall that hosted the likes of Sarah Bernhardt and Maurice Ravel. Inside the building, old architectural styles and themes have been carried over: the use of blue, gray, burgundy, and lilac-colored tiles in Celtic motifs is an example. Care has been taken to maintain the look of Old Montréal from the street, but inside it is almost all new.

From here, you can walk along St-Jacques to rue McGill and turn right to arrive at:

2. place Victoria. Stand in the center of the square beside the fountain, facing the statue of Queen Victoria. The statue of the queen, from whom the square takes its name, was erected here in 1872. Notice that none of the buildings around you is higher than Mont-Royal, which is 763 feet (232½ meters) high. This is not by accident, but by city law. The city's tallest building, 1000 de la Gauchetière (which you'll visit later), for instance, measures 761 feet (232 meters).

To help you get your bearings, scan the scene. To your left is the Stock Exchange Tower (called Tour de la Bourse or Tour de la place Victoria), then 1000 de la Gauchetière. Just below it, you'll spot the IBM Building with its distinctive needle nose. The low brown concrete building is place Bonaventure.

Directly in front of you is the Bell Canada Building and, beside it, stands the taller National Bank of Canada Building, both designed in 1982. The lower skyscraper with its roof painted green to match nearby St-Patrick's Church is the former Air Canada Building.

The art nouveau entrance to the place Victoria metro, created by Hector Guimard for the city of Paris early in the 20th century, was a gift from the city of Paris to the city of Montréal in 1966.

Now that you've got your bearings a bit, go inside the building to your left, the 47-story, earthquake-proof:

3. Stock Exchange Tower, designed by the Italian architects Luigi Moretti and Pier Nervi. When it was built in 1964 it was one of the tallest concrete structures (as opposed to steel) in North America. The Bell Canada and National Bank of Canada buildings that you just looked at, for example, are steel structures.

Walk into the building to see the glass chandelier and, in the center of the lobby, the 43-foot (13-meter), four-story-high stalactite made of 3,000 pieces of glass. Both the chandelier and the glass sculpture come from Murano, Italy.

From here, you may walk through the Radisson Hotel (follow the pathway past the restaurant and escalator and out the main entrance) or walk outside along rue St-Antoine to the corner of rue University. From this corner, take a moment to look back at the architecture of the Radisson: the crenellated facade, the revolving restaurant on top, and the three banks of elevators with views of the modern city.

Cross rues St-Antoine and University to enter:

4. place Bonaventure, at 825 rue University, the first large exposition hall in the city. Built from 1966 to 1967, it gives new meaning to the term multifunctional, hosting more than 60 major consumer exhibitions and trade shows a year. It was built over and around the city's central railway lines, so that trains actually go through the building to get to Windsor Station on the other side.

The place Bonaventure metro station was completed at the same time as the place Bonaventure complex. The complex consists of two floors of shops, offices, exhibition rooms, an underground parking garage for 1,000 cars, and the 450-room Bonaventure Hilton hotel.

Inside, take the elevator to the "RC" (it stands for *rez-de-chaussée,* or ground floor), then follow the "Metro" signs, though you won't actually take it (basically, you'll take a left, then go to the Exposition Hall, then right at the shops). Turn left at the information kiosk.

At the end of this hallway you can exit to the street (you'll be at rue Mansfield at de la Gauchetière), but I recommend taking the elevator on your right to the Bonaventure Hilton hotel lobby. Get off at the 17th floor, and walk to the window for a view of the city.

As you gaze out from here, look for the copper domes at each corner of 1000 de la Gauchetière, directly in front of you. They are purposefully reminiscent of the domes atop Cathédrale Marie-Reine-du-Monde (a replica of Saint Peter's in Rome), to the right. Note also that most of the buildings around the park, called place du Canada, are gray with green touches. Again, no accident. Below the IBM-Marathon Building, with its distinctive point on top, you'll see the Gothic Revival–style St-George's Anglican Church (1870), on rue Peel.

Take a look at the model of place Bonaventure near the window. It shows in detail the complex's trains, exhibition halls, offices, hotel, and cinemas. Such multifunctional space keeps downtown Montréal lively and safe, city developers believe, since something is always going on. This must be reassuring to the 60,000 people who live downtown.

From the window, walk down the short hallway to the hotel lobby for a look at the rooftop pool and gardens. If the door is open, stroll through the gardens and commune with the squirrels, ducks, goldfish, and birds, fed by a conscientious gardener. This is a true hidden oasis in the city. The lively interior of the hotel certainly contrasts with its stark concrete exterior.

REFUELING STOP If you want to rest your feet at this point, consider a drink in the Bonaventure Hilton's lobby bar or its **Bar Soleil.**

Exit the hotel onto Mansfield and walk to de la Gauchetière. Turn left and cross rue Mansfield. You'll see the reflection of Cathédrale Marie-Reine-du-Monde, built in the late 19th century, in the facade of:

5. 1000 de la Gauchetière. Enter the building and take the escalator up. Walk behind the reception desk, past the elevator bank, to the indoor skating rink. It's said that Montréalers are born on skates, and they can indulge their love for the invigorating activity here year round, even on their lunch hour (look for the guys in jackets and ties).

An enormous skylight floats above the rink and a food court circles it. The space is called the Bell Amphitheater, and sometimes the ice is removed, chairs are brought in, and shows take place here.

When you take the escalator back to the street, you'll get an IMAX-type view of the cathedral. When you walk out of the building, look to your left for a fine view of the distinctive needlenose:

6. IBM-Marathon Building, designed by the New York firm of Kohn, Pederson, and Fox and built in 1991. The building is made of granite and glass, and while it is the same height as the 51-story 1000 de la Gauchetière, it has only 47 stories. (Can you figure out what the difference is?)

The point on top, for decoration only, draws attention to the building, and when you walk inside (which you won't do on this tour), you'll enter a 82-foot (25 meter-) high atrium. Note how sleek the building, a joint venture of IBM and Marathon Realties (a subsidiary of Canadian Pacific), looks in comparison to the boxy architecture of the buildings to the right of it, the green Laurentian Bank Building and the taller Imperial Bank of Commerce Building.

Cross de la Gauchetière and go directly into the park. Or if you want to exert a little more energy and enjoy a memorable view, you can cross de la Cathédrale and go up the fairly steep stainless-steel stairway outside place du Canada, an office complex next to the Château Champlain hotel, an innovative concrete structure built from 1964 to 1967 to accommodate visitors to Expo '67.

The hotel's half-moon-shaped windows copy those of Windsor Station. The Château Champlain was designed by Jean-Paul Pothier and Roger d'Astous, the latter a student of Frank Lloyd Wright.

The pedestrian walkway over de la Gauchetière will deposit you in place du Canada. Walk through it to boulevard René-Lévesque.

The building across the street and to your right, topped by a Canadian flag, may not be so modern (it's beaux arts style), but it is significant. The:

7. Sun Life Building, on rue Metcalfe facing Dorchester Square, was the largest building in the British Commonwealth when it was constructed, in three stages, from 1914 to 1931. Called "the Wedding Cake," it reigned for decades as the most impressive building in Canada, with its classical design and Corinthian and Ionic columns. If you stroll by at 5pm you'll hear the sound of chimes emanating from it.

Directly across Dorchester Square from the Sun Life Building stands the streamlined:

8. Banque du Commerce, formerly the Canadian Imperial Bank of Commerce, built from 1959 to 1962. This was one of the first modern office towers in Montréal to be built solely by a Canadian architect, Peter Dickinson. The window rails are made of slate, an unusual touch for a skyscraper, to complement the glass and stainless steel typical of so many modern buildings.

At boulevard René-Lévesque, turn right and walk past Mary, Queen of the World Cathedral. Cross the street at rue Mansfield to visit:

9. place Ville-Marie, known simply as "PVM" to Montréalers. The multifunctional PVM complex, made up of four buildings around an open plaza, was originally inspired in 1930 by Rockefeller Center in New York City and was to have been four times larger. The complex was developed by William Zeckendorf and influenced the design of many downtown areas throughout Canada in the 1960s.

The majestic 42-story building on the plaza, the Royal Bank of Canada, was the first to be built and is the biggest and the most impressive of the four buildings. Designed by I. M. Pei and constructed between 1959 and 1962, it was the city's first modern skyscraper, and it changed the face of downtown Montréal forever. The building's cross shape is reminiscent of the cross atop Mont-Royal; the beacon on top, the symbol of the bank, can be seen for 50 miles; and the three flags flying outside the building represent Québec, Montréal, and place Ville-Marie.

The Underground City started here, when the building's basement was turned into shops and linked by underground passageways to the Queen Elizabeth Hotel (1958) across the street and Windsor Station beyond it.

Walk across the plaza to the fountain, called *Female Landscape,* by sculptor Gerald Gladstone of Toronto. Thirty-six feet (10 meters) in diameter, it recycles 160,000 gallons of water per hour, except when temperatures drop below 15 degrees below zero.

Beyond the fountain, you can look out at:

10. avenue McGill College, which was laid out in the 1840s on land donated by James McGill (for whom the university, founded in 1821, is named). For almost 60 years architects and city planners (the French architect Jacques Greber, Hugh Jones, and I. M. Pei, among them) had talked of widening the avenue to provide more visibility. (Try to imagine what it must have been like before this improvement: a sliver of a street with narrow sidewalks.) But in 1983, "progress" almost blotted Mont-Royal from the urban landscape altogether. The Québec government had authorized the construction of a concert hall on avenue McGill College, which would have blocked the view of the mountain as well as changed the special ambience of the avenue. There was an enormous public outcry (Montréalers are partial to their mountain and feel reassured to see it at every possible opportunity; it is, after all, one of the elements that makes their city unique), and the project was scrapped.

The widening of the avenue came about when a consortium of building owners along the avenue and representatives of the City of Montréal contracted local architect Peter Rose to do the work in 1987. The project was completed in 1989.

To the left of the avenue, you can see a brick and blue-green building, place Montréal Trust, a shopping complex filled with trendy boutiques. To the right is the BNP, or National Bank of Paris, built in 1981.

REFUELING STOP   This is a good place to stop for a coffee or lunch break because **Le Commensal** is nearby, at 1204 avenue McGill College (at rue Ste-Catherine). It serves fresh, superb vegetarian fare—soups, salads, hot and cold main dishes, hot side dishes, tofu prepared several ways, and a bevy of desserts. It's cafeteria-style, so help yourself, then pay by weight (the food's, not your own). The second-floor location affords a good view of avenue McGill College.

From the PVM plaza, go down the steps located just beyond the fountain, cross rue Cathcart and walk up avenue McGill College to the first street, rue Ste-Catherine, where you will turn right and walk to rue University. You'll see the Gothic Revival–style Christ Church Cathedral in front of a 34-story pink skyscraper called:

11. place de la Cathédrale. Notice the Gothic-style windows at the top of the building—a bow to the Anglican cathedral (1856–59) below. The cathedral was sinking (in fact, its 127-foot aluminum-covered steel steeple replaces a heavier stone one that had lapsed into a perilous tilt), and the steel, stone, and glass skyscraper and underground shops built here from 1985 to 1988 actually shore it up.

In the year 2,063, ownership of the skyscraper and the underground complex will revert to the church, which donated the land on which they are built and gave the developers a truly long-term lease. The church's old rectory was moved stone-by-stone to make way for the skyscraper and is now a restaurant in the same block.

The Cloister Garden of the place de la Cathédrale provides a welcoming downtown green space and is designed like a medieval cloister garden, with covered walkways and hedge-enclosed grass beds arranged geometrically around a central fountain.

Walk into the courtyard and then into the lobby of the building, where you'll see that the architecture of the cathedral is reflected in more ways than one. The shopping concourse on the lower level, Promenades de la Cathédrale, is directly underneath the cathedral, which rested on supporting beams in the middle of an excavated hole for many months while it was being constructed.

Walk through the lobby and exit onto rue de Maisonneuve, where you will turn left. At avenue McGill College, turn right. You'll pass more modern buildings, including 1801 avenue McGill College, and in the middle of the block on the left-hand side of the street, at 2000 avenue McGill College, La Tour L'Industriele Vie. Complete your walk in front of the arresting:

12. *The Illuminated Crowd,* a sculpture of people in various attitudes by the British sculptor Raymond Mason. The sculpture looks as if it were carved from butter but in fact is made of plastic painted a pale yellow. Look carefully at the faces, especially toward the back, where you'll find folks in dire straits and even a sinister masked man with a dagger. Viewers have speculated that the crowd is gazing up at a fire . . . or at fireworks. To me, they are marveling at the modern city that has sprung up on the soil that once nourished an Amerindian community called Hochelaga.

The sculpture stands in front of the:

13. Laurentian Bank Building, at 1981 avenue McGill College, home of the Laurentian Bank and the National Bank of Paris. The accordion-like complex, with its glass facade, is made up of 16- and 20-story towers and a 36-foot- (11-meter-high) lobby with granite and steel decoration that accentuates its vertical lines.

REFUELING STOP From here, it couldn't be more convenient (if it's lunch or dinner time) to sample the upbeat ambience at **Baci,** an Italian restaurant at 2095 avenue McGill College. It's got a contemporary triple-level design (no Chianti bottles anywhere); efficient service; soft piano music in the evening; and, last but most important, stellar cuisine, mostly northern Italian, with a creative spin. They'll even prepare risotto at night, if you're willing to wait 45 minutes for it. The McGill University campus is right across the street.

This marks the official end of the modern architecture tour, but I highly recommend one more stop, if there's time in your day—a visit to the:

14. Canadian Centre for Architecture (CCA), at 1920 rue Baile, a 20-minute walk southeast or a quick metro ride away (take the McGill metro to the Guy-Concordia stop). It's both a

PHYLLIS LAMBERT

Director and founder of the Canadian Centre for Architecture, Phyllis Lambert, a native of Montréal, is well known for her contribution to contemporary architecture and her concern for urban conservation. Lambert is the founding president of Heritage Montréal (1975) and was instrumental in founding (and is now president of) the Société du Patrimoine Urbain de Montréal in 1979. From 1980 to 1983, the Société established the largest nonprofit cooperative-housing renovation project in Canada, enabling an entire neighborhood (Milton-Park, north of downtown Montréal) to survive without gentrification.

An undergraduate of Vassar College, Lambert obtained a masters degree in architecture from the Illinois Institute of Technology in Chicago. Lambert was director of planning for the Seagram Building in New York (1954–58). She designed the Saidye Bronfman Center in Montréal (1964–67), and she was the architect and developer for the renovation of the Biltmore Hotel in Los Angeles (1978).

The recipient of many titles and honors, Lambert was awarded the Gold Medal of the Royal Architectural Institute of Canada in 1991, the highest professional honor in architecture in Canada. In 1992, she was named an officer of the Ordre des Arts et Lettres by the French government for her efforts to preserve Montréal's architectural heritage and for founding the Canadian Centre for Architecture.

research center and a museum with changing exhibits that explore the history, the art, and the impact of architecture.

The CCA incorporates the Second Empire–style Shaughnessy House (1874), framed but not daunted by a modern building (1985–88) designed by Montréal architect Peter Rose with Phyllis Lambert. The marriage of the two buildings is a modern-architecture success story. The presence of the CCA has greatly invigorated the neighborhood where it is located, one that had been devastated by the widening of boulevard René-Lévesque and the addition of underpasses and entrance and exit ramps for the Ville-Marie Highway.

The buildings, old and new, and the unique CCA Garden

across the street make the trip here worthwhile, but you'll be triply blessed if you take time to visit the extensive bookstore and see the exhibits (there is an admission charge for the latter.)

From here, return to the Guy-Concordia metro station, or take a taxi to your hotel or next destination.

PETER ROSE

Born in Montréal in 1943, Peter Rose received both a bachelor's and master's degree in architecture from Yale University and has been an adjunct professor of architecture in the Graduate School of Design at Harvard University since 1991. Rose is the principal in Peter Rose Architect, the company he established in Montréal in 1974, and he designed the master plan for the Old Port in Montréal; Eaton Centre; and the Canadian Centre for Architecture, which received the Prix d'Excellence from the Ordre des Architects du Québec in 1989 and a design award from the American Institute of Architects in 1992.

A Shopper's Walk

Start: The Bay.
Finish: Holt Renfrew.
Time: 1½ to 2 hours (not including actual shopping; that's up to you).
Metro: McGill College.
Best Time: Weekday mornings from 10am on, or after 2pm, when the streets hum with big-city vibrancy but aren't crowded with lunch-hour shoppers. Note that stores tend to close at 5pm Monday through Wednesday and Saturday; they stay open later (to 9pm) on Thursday and Friday.
Worst Time: Sundays, when some stores are closed.

Montréal is a city with a flair for fashion and one of the great fashion capitals of the world, with more than 1,500 businesses involved in the manufacturing of clothing as well as two schools of fashion, LaSalle College and Collège Marie-Victorin. In this city, the attention paid to style and fashion is apparent immediately. You'll see well-turned-out women, men, and young people everywhere. They make style look so easy.

World-renowned fashion labels, as well as the creations of

Montréal's own well-known designers and some of its rising stars—between 15 and 20 designers or their labels are household words here—are sold in its grand department stores as well as in some specialty boutiques. But it's the department stores that are most visible in downtown Montréal, and so much a fabric of daily life here. Young Montréalers frequent them religiously, just as their parents and grandparents did.

Most of the department stores were founded when Scottish, Irish, and English families dominated the city's commerce, and so their names remain Anglophone (except La Baie/The Bay, which goes both ways), even though their merchandise and appeal are unquestionably bilingual.

Most of Montréal's department stores are strung along rue Ste-Catherine from Phillips Square at rue Aylmer west to rue Guy, a 12-block stretch that makes for a straightforward walking tour that can keep a serious shopper busy for quite some time. This is a great rainy-day tour because the major shopping complexes are linked via a network of underground passageways known collectively as the Underground City and encompassing some 1,700 shops.

If you plan to do some shopping on this tour (I'd be surprised if you didn't, because it certainly offers every opportunity), first pay a visit to a bank to exchange your own currency for Canadian dollars as banks give a better rate than department stores. You should also note that a number of the big stores in Montréal issue their own charge cards.

The McGill College stop on the metro will deposit you in the basement of:

1. The Bay (La Baie), short for the Hudson's Bay Company, on rue Ste-Catherine near rue Aylmer. In one form or another this company has been doing business in Canada for the better part of 400 years. The Scotsman Henry Morgan first set up shop in Old Montréal in 1843, in a store called Smith & Morgan that he ran with David Smith, who was replaced as a partner in 1852 by Henry's brother James. In 1855, the store, by then called Henry Morgan & Company, moved to rue McGill College and Victoria Square; in 1891 it took up residence in its present home on rue Ste-Catherine in downtown Montréal in a four-story, red sandstone (imported from England) building known as Colonial House.

By 1902 the store had added a fifth story; another three stories followed in 1923, at which time the facade was also moved out 350 feet (107 meters) along rue Union. The store was enlarged once more in 1964, along rue Maisonneuve. Escalators

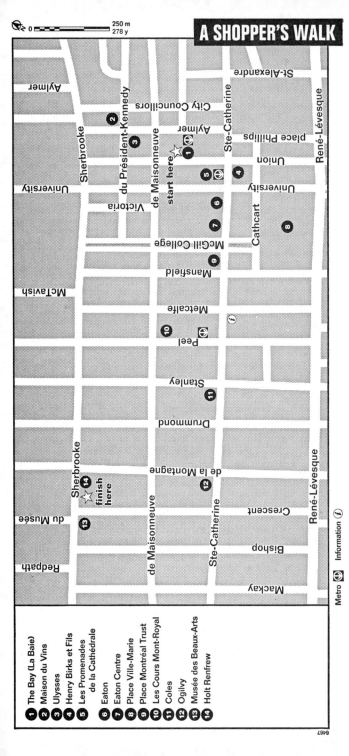

A SHOPPER'S WALK

0   250 m
          278 y

1. The Bay (La Baie)
2. Maison du Vins
3. Ulysses
4. Henry Birks et Fils
5. Les Promenades
   de la Cathédrale
6. Eaton
7. Eaton Centre
8. Place Ville-Marie
9. Place Montréal Trust
10. Les Cours Mont-Royal
11. Coles
12. Ogilvy
13. Musée des Beaux-Arts
14. Holt Renfrew

Metro   Information

6467

weren't added until 1946. And it wasn't until 1972 that the venerable Morgans became The Bay.

The Bay's main store is a full-selection department store in every sense, but the emphasis historically was on furs and warm wool products for the chilly Québec winters. Today, its newly remodeled fashion floors sell all of the major international designers, as well as local Québécois couturiers.

From The Bay, walk up rue Aylmer to avenue du Président-

MARIE SAINT PIERRE

Described as young, upbeat, and delightfully offbeat (*"flyée"* in French), Marie Saint Pierre struck out on her own as a designer in 1986, after only a few months working in the fashion industry in Montréal, armed with a diploma from the city's Lasalle College and *beaucoup* self-confidence. That year her fall line of coats was sold in upscale boutiques, and the designs drew praise and sales for their originality, cut, and quality.

In 1988, Marie Saint Pierre created a ready-to-wear collection that was sold throughout Québec, and the following year she was chosen as the first designer from Québec to participate in the Fashion Coterie of New York. Her clothes began showing up in boutiques in SoHo, and *Women's Wear Daily* published an article on her. In the 1990s, the magazine *Chatelaine* selected Marie Saint Pierre as one of Québec's up-and-coming women, and her clothes were featured in a television ad campaign for Eaton Centre.

Marie Saint Pierre's clothes are often long and fluid in style, with unusual details, such as hand-embroidered collars made from fabric scraps; handmade wooden or horn buttons; and uneven hems, some reminiscent of the pointed edges of leaves. The details are subtle and often abstract, and the designs combine the creative touch of the artisan with modern fabrics.

Today her label is sold in New York, Paris, and throughout Canada. In Montréal, she is represented at La Baie and Holt Renfrew and in the Marie Saint Pierre boutique at 4455 rue St-Denis. The designer's hand can also be seen in the uniforms worn by the staffs of Montréal's Museum of Contemporary Art, Biodome, and Planetarium.

Kennedy, cross the street, and enter the modern building with the red entrance at 505 avenue du Président-Kennedy. Inside and to your right is the large and impressive:

2. **Maison du Vins.** This gourmet grocery store for wines has 3,000 bottles imported from 55 countries. You can spend $10 for a bottle or over $1,000—if your taste runs to Château Petrus 1971, that is. In the same building, but across the hall from the wine store, is an equally inviting gourmet enterprise called The Cheese Shoppe, whose wares complement wine perfectly.

Across the street and cater-corner to the wine and cheese shops, at 560 avenue du Président-Kennedy, stands Montréal's famous travel bookstore:

3. **Ulysses,** which carries a good selection of travel books and guidebooks, many in English, and travel accessories like money pouches, pill cases, day packs, and sewing kits. If you need anything, here's your chance to get it. (A small branch of this bookstore is also found in the Ogilvy department store.)

Walk back along rue Aylmer, go right on Ste-Catherine, and walk to the corner of Union. Overlooking Phillips Square is Montréal's answer to Tiffany's:

4. **Henry Birks et Fils,** facing Christ Church Cathedral. This beautiful old store, with its dark-wood display cases, marble pillars and floors, and ornate ceiling decoration, is a living part of Montréal's Victorian heritage. John Birks and his wife left their native England in 1840 for Canada, where their son, Henry, was born. On March 1, 1879, Henry founded the company that still bears his name on rue St-Jacques, at the site where the Royal Bank stands today.

In 1894, when Montréal's population numbered 328,000, the store moved to its Phillips Square location. The building you see today is the product of two expansions, one in 1902 and the second in 1906, when the red sandstone facade was extended 200 feet (61 meters). Entering its second century, Birks will no doubt continue to be the symbol of *bon goût* (good taste) for Montréalers.

Birks is known for fine jewelry and high-quality gift items. Wander through the displays of jewelry, crystal and porcelain, pens and desk accessories, watches, ties, leather goods, belts and other accessories, and artistic stoneware, for a look at the finer things in life.

From Birks, you'll follow rue Ste-Catherine, undeniably a shopper's street, filled with department stores, a multistory shopping complex, and plenty of small shops. If you enter the metro stop at place de la Cathédrale, you'll discover:

5. les Promenades de la Cathédrale. One hundred shops on two levels here are filled with clothing, accessories, jewelry, and gifts. The location is undeniably unique: under Christ Church Cathedral. The shopping development, anchored into bedrock 60 feet below street level, actually shores up the cathedral, which had started to sink under its own weight as far back as 1927.

At 677 rue Ste-Catherine and rue University stands:

6. Eaton, Montréal's largest store. The first Eaton store was opened by Timothy Eaton in Toronto in 1869. It was another 56 years before the company would open a store—this one—in Montréal. The building was designed by the architecture firm of Ross & MacDonald, and another three floors were added in 1930.

The art deco restaurant Le 9e (modern for its day) on the top floor was designed by Jacques Carlu, who studied in Paris and worked in the United States. Carlu fashioned the restaurant after the dining room of the ocean liner *Ile de France*. (See "Refueling Stop," below, for more information.)

REFUELING STOP You've probably never been to a restaurant quite like **Le 9e**—the name refers to the ninth (*le neuvième*) floor of Eaton, where it's located—unless you've eaten in the dining room of a cruise liner. One has been re-created here and has been permanently in port at Eaton's since 1931. Some of the wait staff have been around nearly that long, which adds to the appeal and the kitschiness. Le 9e is a good, though sometimes noisy, choice for lunch or dessert. Make this a port of call on your walking tour, even if you don't dine here.

For a vegetarian meal or snack in a pleasant setting, head to the health-conscious **Le Commensal,** 1204 avenue McGill College between rues Ste-Catherine and Cathcart. It's on the second floor and has a long picture window overlooking the street. The hot and cold fare features a large assortment of good cooking, served cafeteria-style.

Next door to Eaton on rue Ste-Catherine is the five-story:

7. Eaton Centre, which has no relation to the department store except in name. Built in 1990, it is the largest shopping complex in the downtown area, consisting of an atrium; 225 splashy, upscale boutiques; and a popular multiscreen cinema on the top level. At Christmas time, the head and front feet of a giant reindeer protrude from Eaton Centre's facade.

From Eaton Centre, continue on Ste-Catherine to avenue

TIMOTHY EATON

Born in Ireland in 1834, Timothy Eaton left school when he was 13 to work as an apprentice in a small general store. When he was 20, he immigrated to Canada, where he would one day make retailing history. Fifteen years after he arrived, in 1869, he opened the first Eaton store, in Toronto. In 1884 he published his first mail order catalog: A mere 32 pages, it would mushroom over the years into a colorful, 400-page biannual tome. (Like the late-lamented Sear's catalog in the United States, Eaton's catalog is no more, having ceased publication in 1976.)

In the late 19th century, Eaton's catalog was required reading for immigrants bound for Canada; besides selling them ready-to-assemble homes and schools, it revealed much to them about life in their adoptive homeland. The catalog brought the company welcome revenue and the wherewithal to expand. By 1886 Eaton was operating its own factories and producing garments sold only at its store—the first Canadian store to do so. By 1907, the year that Timothy Eaton died, his company had its own private label.

It wasn't until 1925 that an Eaton store opened in Montréal, and it remains the city's largest department store.

Eaton set countrywide work standards over the years. It was the first store in Canada to set shorter working hours, the first to introduce employee holidays, and the first to continue paying wages to employees fighting in World Wars I and II.

McGill College and take a left. If you follow avenue McGill College south one short block you'll come to a set of steps that lead to the city's first big shopping complex, and the first building block in its now mammoth Underground City:

8. **place Ville-Marie** (PVM for short), built in 1962. Beneath the towering cross-shaped structure (the Royal Bank of Canada Building), you'll discover a shopping promenade with 100 boutiques and specialty stores, linked via handy passageways to still more shops in other downtown shopping complexes.

Return to rue Ste-Catherine and avenue McGill College to delve deeper into shoppers' terrain at:

9. **place Montreal Trust,** which fills the block and accommodates 120 boutiques and specialty shops on five levels linked by

THE UNDERGROUND CITY

Snow, sleet, rain, or sweltering heat—Montréalers can cope because they can shop in the Underground City, where it's dry and temperature-controlled year-round. When place Ville-Marie rose on the downtown skyline in 1962, underground shops were installed on its two lower levels and connected to the nearby Queen Elizabeth Hotel and Windsor Station. That was just the beginning.

Today, 18 miles (29 kilometers) of underground passageways link shopping complexes and department stores galore, not to mention hotels, cinemas, and exhibition halls. And each year city planners just keep adding more to the network.

If you're a novice to the Underground City, finding your way around can be confusing, since there's no predictable grid to help you along. So prepare to get lost, stumble upon unexpected finds, and enjoy the adventure of it all.

escalators and elevators. Built in 1989, the modern complex has a large atrium, a multitiered fountain, and a glass wall that lets the sun shine in from avenue McGill College. At Christmas time, a 63-foot-high tree fills the atrium.

At rues Mansfield and Ste-Catherine is the site of a former department store, Simpson's. It closed in 1990. Bloomingdale's was reportedly considering taking over the space, but it didn't. Hopefully, when you pass by, it will have been reincarnated into another grand store.

Around the corner from rue Ste-Catherine on rue Metcalfe is the ever-helpful Infotouriste, so if you need maps or information of any kind, take a short detour here. You actually can do some shopping there, too, since there is a small bookstore on the premises featuring guide- and coffee-table books about Montréal and Québec.

Continue along rue Ste-Catherine one block to rue Peel. If you turn right and walk to the end of the block you'll arrive at:

10. **Les Cours Mont-Royal,** at 1455 rue Peel. The old Mount Royal Hotel, built in 1922, was transformed through careful renovation into this elegant downtown shopping complex that opened in 1988. Four levels here house 100 boutiques, restau-

rants, and a cinema, and there are also two seven-floor office towers and condominiums in the complex.

Back on rue Ste-Catherine, walk to the corner of rue Stanley and admire the city's largest bookstore:

11. Coles, at 1171 rue Ste-Catherine. The store, which has been renovated and expanded to twice its original size, opened here in 1976. It is part of the Coles Bookstore chain, which claims some 240 stores across Canada (the first opened in Toronto in 1934). This stellar Coles store has 20,000 square feet of space devoted to books and spreads over three floors.

Attention to detail is apparent in the interior's marble floors and wooden trim, and in the third-floor atrium with wrought-iron railing and lampposts that overlooks the second floor. Weary browsers may linger in a window seat or on a park bench that's come in from the cold.

This Coles store has one of the largest selections of English-language titles in Québec, as well as plenty of French books. Among the most extensive selections are Canadian-authored books in English and French, English and French children's books, books of local interest, art books, cookbooks, literature, and poetry. And if you're in the market for magazines, postcards, greeting cards, calendars, or stationery, Coles can supply them, too. The store has a special-order department, so if you can't find what you're looking for, they will try and track it down and mail it to you . . . anywhere in the world.

Continue down rue Ste-Catherine 2 more blocks; at 1307 rue Ste-Catherine and rue de la Montagne stands the upscale:

12. Ogilvy, established by James Angus Ogilvy in 1856. In 1912 his small dry-goods store was replaced by the building you see today (the fifth floor and Tudor Hall concert space were added in 1927 by new owner, Colonel Aird Nesbitt, who ran the store for over 50 years and established its reputation for quality).

Besides fashion, Ogilvy is well-known among Montréalers for its mechanical Christmas windows, a Nesbitt innovation, which have been a gift to the city every year since 1947.

In 1985, the store was bought and renovated over a two-year period by Le Groupe Equidev, a company controlled by Daniel Fournier, a francophone who was a Rhodes scholar and former CFL football player and made his mark in commercial real estate. The store's high-end clothing department, with 20-foot-wide aisles, is now on the elegant third floor.

Even though the store has changed hands, one aspect of it has not changed: You can be assured of hearing the skirl of a

JEAN-CLAUDE POITRAS

Canada's standard bearer for classic, sophisticated fashions for men and women is Jean-Claude Poitras, who was born in Montréal in 1949 and studied at the prestigious art and design school Ecole des Metiers Commerciaux in Montréal. Poitras worked at Eaton as a buyer and boutique director and in 1977 designed his first men's and women's collections under the label Bol. His own label for a women's ready-to-wear line was launched in 1983.

Poitras went on to design accessories, watches, shearling coats, and furs, as well as uniforms for airlines, government agencies, and Montréal's Fine Arts Museum. In 1987 he formed his own company, Poitras Design, which joined forces three years later with Irving Samuel, a fashion house founded in Montréal in 1945. The company now employs 200 people and both labels are sold throughout Canada, the United States, Europe, and Asia.

The winner of numerous design awards over the past 15 years, Poitras was the first North American fashion designer to be invited, in 1991, to Herren Mode Woche, the international menswear fair in Colgne Germany. In 1988, he received the Best Designer Award for both menswear and womenswear at Gala de Mode, the first major event in Québec to recognize the excellence of fashions made in the province.

Poitras's client list reads like a Who's Who of Canadian entertainment, business, and politics. In Montréal, his designs are sold in the Ogilvy, Eaton, Bay, and Holt Renfrew department stores. The Jean-Claude Poitras Boutique, owned by Mr. Poitras, is located on the second floor of Ogilvy.

Scottish piper ringing through Ogilvy every day at opening and closing time.

At rue Crescent, turn right and head 2 blocks up to reach stylish rue Sherbrooke, passing small, exclusive shops selling art, antiques, Armani, and Laura Ashley. It's hard to believe that this stretch of the city was once a run-down slum area, slated for demolition, before investors saw possibilities in these delightful old houses and brought them back to life.

REFUELING STOP For a quiet spot to munch on a croissant or sip some strong coffee, choose **Café Via Crescent,** at 1418 rue Crescent. If you prefer a trendier setting with more action, cross the street and get a sidewalk table (and a beer) at **Sir Winston Churchill Pub,** located at 1459 rue Crescent.

At the corner of rues Crescent and Sherbrooke stands the new addition to the:

13. Musée des Beaux-Arts (Museum of Fine Arts), Canada's oldest and Montréal's finest museum. The modern annex was added in 1991 and is connected to the stately Greek Revival original building (1912) across the street by an underground tunnel/gallery. There is a museum store on the ground floor and a bookstore downstairs; both are closed Monday, when the museum is, except in December.

If you walk west on rue Sherbrooke from here, you'll pass numerous art galleries. If you walk east 1 block, to rue de la Montagne, you'll come to another fine department store, and the end of this tour, the top of the line:

14. Holt Renfrew, at 1300–1312 rue Sherbrooke. What Harrod's is to London or Saks is to New York, Holt Renfrew is to Montréal. Holt's was founded in Québec City in 1837 by William Samuel Henderson, an immigrant from Londonderry, Ireland, who had opened a men's hat shop three years earlier.

In the 1850s, Henderson was bought out by two men who had become his partners, G. R. Renfrew and John Holt, and it was they who established its esteemed reputation in the fur business. Queen Victoria herself was a patron, and in 1948 Holt Renfrew was selected to create a Labrador wild mink coat as Canada's wedding present to Queen Elizabeth II.

Holt opened its first store in Montréal in 1910, and the present store was constructed in 1937 by the architecture firm of Ross & MacDonald, which also designed Eaton. They went in a more modern direction with this building (note the windows), and in 1938 it received the Medal of Honor of the Royal Architectural Institute of Canada.

Holt Renfrew contracted with the House of Dior for the exclusive representation in Canada of its haute couture furs, couture boutique, accessories, and perfume. And it was the first store in North America to represent simultaneously the European fashion designers Yves Saint Laurent, Christian Dior, and Valentino.

In addition to haute clothing for men and women, including the original works of French designers, you'll find furnishings and a food section stocking delicacies like caviar and truffles inside this posh place.

REFUELING STOP If you walk less than a block east from Holt Renfrew, passing the Ralph Lauren shop on your way, you'll arrive at the **Ritz-Carlton** (1228 rue Sherbrooke, at the corner of Drummond). Finding yourself in its intimate bar for tea or a drink is the perfect end to a perfect walk. Put those shopping bags down and relax!

WALKING TOUR 8

Ile Ste-Hélène & Ile Notre-Dame

Start: Information kiosk on Ile Ste-Hélène.
Finish: Beach at Ile Notre-Dame.
Time: 3 to 5 hours.
Metro: Ile Ste-Hélène.
Best Time: During the day, preferably a sunny day, because you'll be outdoors most of the time. If you want to go to La Ronde amusement park, plan to start the tour by 10am; if you want to swim at the beach at the end of this tour be sure to pack your swimsuit and a towel.
Worst Time: A rainy day; you'll get drenched.

Unassuming little Ile Ste-Hélène (St. Helen's Island), which lies offshore from Montréal in the St. Lawrence River, led a quiet existence until the 20th century. The City of Montréal acquired it in 1907 to build a park, but the federal government took it over during World War II for use as a prisoner-of-war camp. Then it changed forever in the 1960's, when it was chosen for the site of Terre des Hommes and the tremendously successful Expo '67. The Montréal

Expo, much like a world's fair, attracted the largest attendance of any exposition in history—53 million people.

In the four years before Expo opened, construction crews reshaped the island and doubled its surface area. They went on to create a brand new island right next to it, called Ile Notre-Dame. Much of the earth needed to build the new island was dredged up from the bed of the St. Lawrence River; additionally, 15 million tons of rock from the excavation of the metro (built around this time) and from the Décarie Expressway was brought in by truck. Bridges were added to link the islands to the mainland and to each other, and 83 pavilions were constructed.

When Expo closed, the city government preserved the site. Parts of it were used for Olympic Games events in 1976, and today people come to enjoy its parks, swimming pools, old fort and the museum it houses, casino, floral gardens, French restaurant, amusement park, and beach. To me, the islands have a real beach-town atmosphere in summer.

When you come out of the metro (there's only one exit), you'll notice three swimming pools and a brownstone building that resembles a monastery but is actually a bathers' pavilion.

To the left of the metro exit, there are some useful orientation panels and an:

1. **information office,** where you can get a handy map. Across from it, in a separate building, is a snack bar, bicycle rental, ice-cream counter, picnic tables, and toilets.

REFUELING STOP If you've arrived hungry, or need a cup of coffee before setting out on your explorations, take advantage of the snack bar here. You can also buy some fruit to carry along with you on your walk.

From here, head for the:
2. **Alexander Calder sculpture,** called *Man*. You can't miss it. It dates from Expo days, and was moved to this site in 1992 as part of Montréal's 350th birthday celebration. The artist's initials on the work look like the work of a branding iron.

From this tranquil spot, the view of the city—both old and modern—is splendid, and a handy illustration shows you exactly which buildings you're admiring.

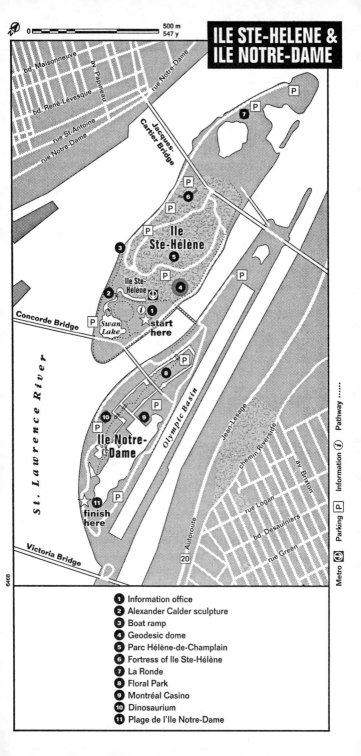

ILE STE-HELENE & ILE NOTRE-DAME

0   500 m
    547 y

Metro Ⓜ   Parking Ⓟ   Information ⓘ   Pathway ......

1 Information office
2 Alexander Calder sculpture
3 Boat ramp
4 Geodesic dome
5 Parc Hélène-de-Champlain
6 Fortress of Ile Ste-Hélène
7 La Ronde
8 Floral Park
9 Montréal Casino
10 Dinosaurium
11 Plage de l'Ile Notre-Dame

Take the path to your right (as you face the city) and walk down to the:

3. boat ramp. This is where the boat from Old Montréal docks (get it at Quai Jacques-Cartier). It runs daily throughout the summer, then on weekends until early October. If you have arrived by boat, you can pick up this walking tour here. From this vantage point, you get a close-up view of the Jacques-Cartier Bridge, the Molson brewery, and the old clock tower.

From the boat ramp, walk along the road that follows the river. You'll pass beneath the Calder sculpture for a different view of it. There are benches here where you can sit and enjoy the river.

Just beyond the sculpture, take the stairs up. You'll see two small bridges arching in front of you. Walk to the center of the first one. The Calder will be on your left, and a geodesic dome will be in front of you.

To your right is the Concorde Bridge and Place des Nations amphitheater (imagine the crowds assembled here for events associated with Expo '67 and the '76 Olympics). Swan Lake (Lac des Cygnes) is in front of the amphitheater.

As you proceed to the second bridge, you'll see Yves

JACQUES-CARTIER BRIDGE

The Harbor Bridge opened officially on May 24, 1930, linking Montréal with Ile Ste-Hélène and the community of Longueuil, on the south shore of the St. Lawrence River. Four years later it was renamed the Jacques-Cartier Bridge, in honor of the 400th anniversary of Cartier's arrival in New France.

The bridge is a beloved symbol to Montréalers, much like the Brooklyn Bridge is to New Yorkers. Its sweep across the St. Lawrence is a familiar and reassuring sight from Old Montréal and the Old Port and from the islands of Ste-Hélène and Notre-Dame.

During the summer fireworks exhibition at La Ronde, the amusement park at the tip of Ile Ste-Hélène, some Montréalers choose to watch the show from the bridge, which is closed to traffic at that time. With a Walkman, viewers can listen to the accompanying music, which is broadcast live from La Ronde.

Trudeau's black sculpture *Cosmos Beacon* to your right. (From another vantage point, it looks a bit like a somewhat startled person peering out at the world. Cross the second bridge, turn right onto the path, and walk toward the geodesic dome.

To help you get an idea of what's in store for you on this tour, gaze straight ahead: You're going to explore the wooded park on the hill to the left of the dome, and perhaps eat at the outstanding French restaurant (see Refueling Stop, below) near the tower with the triangle on top (that's Levis water tower, built in 1936).

To the left of the tower, hidden from view but in the shadow of the Jacques-Cartier Bridge, there's a historical fort that now houses a military museum. To the right of the dome is the bridge that will take you to Ile Notre-Dame; the metro station is in front of the dome.

Before you head off toward the dome, the next stop on this tour, you might want to make a short detour across the small bridge on the left side of the path you're now on. If you do, you'll be rewarded with a fine view of (and photo-op for) the Calder sculpture. A bit farther along this path, you'll discover some colorful. . . . Can you guess what they are? (Please touch.)

Make your way back to the buildings housing the information office and snack bar. Pass them (keeping the metro to your left), and proceed to the larger-than-life:

4. geodesic dome, the former American Pavilion for Expo '67, designed by Buckminster Fuller. The largest geodesic dome in the world, it has a diameter of 250 feet. The acrylic shell that once covered it burned in 1976 and was never replaced. In 1995, the dome will be filled with activity, when it becomes an interpretation center for water and the environment.

REFUELING STOP Behind the dome is **Restaurant Hélène-de-Champlain,** a fairly formal French restaurant (no shorts, please) that has been on the island since 1967. It's particularly popular with the business-lunch crowd, and the lunch special represents good value for money; servings are generous.

Turn left at the dome to enter what I think is the city's prettiest, if unsung, park:

5. Parc Hélène-de-Champlain. The park delineates the original limits of Ile Ste-Hélène before landfill (amazing difference, isn't it?). Take some time to explore it on your own, including the old blockhouse (1848), now used as an observation deck. The pathways lead through woods filled with vegetation indigenous to the area.

From the park, follow a path that leads downhill, towards the Jacques-Cartier Bridge, to the:

6. Fortress of Ile Ste-Hélène, which now houses the David M. Stewart Museum (signs will point you to it). The fort was built between 1820 and 1824 on orders from the Duke of Wellington, who anticipated an attack from the United States, and it was used as a munitions depot.

The walls, made of a red stone quarried on the island, are 3 to 10 feet (1 to 3 meters) thick, with hand-hewn granite corners. A moat surrounds the fort on three sides, and the fast-flowing river protects the exposed side, which faces the city.

It's worth the stroll over to the fort, even if you don't want to pay to go inside. However, if you do go in, you'll see the arsenal, storage shed, barracks (which were partially destroyed by fire in 1875), powder magazine, and blockhouse.

In summer, military life of the 17th and 18th centuries is revisited here: The Compagnie Franche de la Marine, dressed like the troops who protected French outposts in the New World from 1683 to 1760, show off their skills with fixed bayonets, and the kilted Fraser Highlanders carry out drills to the refrain of bagpipes.

From the David M. Stewart Museum, you can walk for 10 minutes past the Jacques-Cartier Bridge (watch for the signs), to arrive at one of the biggest attractions of a Montréal summer:

7. La Ronde. This amusement park fills the northern reaches of Ile Ste-Hélène with 35 rides, family entertainment, an international circus, fireworks, and the tallest double-track roller coaster in the world (it reaches heights of 132 feet and speeds of more than 60 mph).

The International Fireworks Competition is held here every year, beginning in late May or early June and continuing until early August. The amusement park is open daily in summer from 11am to midnight (1am on Friday and Saturday), and on weekends only in May and September.

Make your way back to the fort, through Parc Hélène-de-Champlain, to the geodesic dome. Continue past it to the bridge, on your left, leading to Ile Notre-Dame (just follow the signs for the casino). Bus 167 will also take you to Ile Notre-Dame from the dome.

Cross the bridge and turn right; there is no pedestrian path so watch for cars on the road. You'll walk through gardens and pass a paddleboat-rental kiosk. When you get to a brick walkway, you've arrived at the beautiful:

8. Floral Park (Jardins des Floralies), which will warm the heart of any amateur gardener or botanical garden fan. The gardens were established in 1980 for an international floral exhibition, Les Floralies Internationales, held here for the first time outside of Europe. Lovely remnants from that event remain: The gardens from Great Britain, France, Belgium, and Italy fill this part of the island with the beauty of roses, lilacs, begonias, and a variety of ornamental trees.

The floral park is lined on either side by a canal, navigable by canoe or pedalboat. If you plan to walk back this way (your other alternative is to take the bus back from the final stop), you can explore the gardens on the lefthand side now, and do those on the other side on your way back. If not, your only course is to zigzag back and forth in order to see everything.

The rose garden, part of the Great Britain Garden, was dedicated in 1980 to the Queen Mother on her 80th birthday. One section of it is the illustrated history of the rose, with varieties that have thrilled people throughout the centuries. It also contains the first hybrid tea rose, created in 1867 and called La France (it's at the height of its beauty in September). Expect to see roses with every conceivable name, from Mischief to Schoolgirl.

Next to the Great Britain Garden is the French Garden, which won the grand prize at the Floralies. It was created to display the diverse flora of France by French landscape architect Serge Chateil, with help from the cities of Lyon, Orleans, Hyères, Marseille, Nice, and Paris. The garden incorporates a wooden footbridge, a waterfall, and a small fountain with four female figures holding a crown (a gift from the city of Paris).

The French Garden fronts Montréal's splashy new gaming establishment, the:

9. Montréal Casino, Canada's largest casino, which opened in October of 1993. This striking pennant-capped spiral of a building first welcomed people as the French Pavilion at Expo '67 and was designed by Parisian architects Jean Faugeron and André de Mot. After Expo, it remained an exhibition space, most notably from 1985 to 1992 when it housed the Palais de la Civilisation, site of blockbuster exhibitions on subjects as diverse as China, Ramses, and the cinema.

The daily attendance at the casino is an estimated 5,000 people, who may bet 25¢ to $500 at a time—or just observe the

HELENE DE CHAMPLAIN

In 1610, a young Parisian girl, Hélène Boullé, was contracted in marriage to Samuel de Champlain. She was 12 years old; he was about 40, and had founded Québec City two years earlier. She was a Protestant who converted to Catholicism, his religion, and her dowry helped finance some of his forays into the New World. Champlain named Ile Ste-Hélène after his wife.

The couple began to live together when she reached the legal age of 14, although she continued to live in France until 1620 while her husband made excursions to and from the New World. When Hélène did come to New France with Champlain, she found it a harsh and difficult place in which to live, especially in comparison to the life she was used to. After four years, she returned to France and never saw the colony again.

When Champlain died, in 1635, Hélène became a nun and entered the Ursuline convent in Paris.

scene. Some 1,700 people can play at any given time on 1,200 slot machines and 65 gaming tables.

REFUELING STOP Across from the French Garden and the casino is the casual **Café Terrasse Fleur de l'Ile** housing both a snack bar and a restaurant. International cuisine is served here and it is open daily. If you stop in on a Friday or Saturday evening, you can enjoy dining and dancing.

Cross the small bridge in front of the café. On your right is:
10. **Dinasaurium,** a theme park devoted to the mysteries and marvels of dinosaurs and the earth as it existed for them 200 million years ago. The complex also has hands-on exhibits and a theater showing films about dinosaurs. It was not open at this writing, but is supposed to open in 1994.
   Continue along the path, following the signs for:
11. **Plage de l'Ile Notre-Dame,** a city beach at its best—large, clean, and inviting. The beach is the former Regatta Lake from Expo '67, and water for it is drawn from the Lachine Rapids and treated by a mostly natural filtration system of sand, aquatic

plants, ultraviolet light, and a bit of chlorine to make it safe for swimming. The beach opened in 1991, the dream child of Mayor Jean Doré.

There's a pavilion here with a fast-food eatery and changing facilities inside. There is an admission charge.

At the bus stop near the beach, you can wait for bus 167, or retrace your path back through the gardens to Ile Ste-Hélène and the metro.

WALKING TOUR 9

Plateau Mont-Royal

Start: The corner of Mont-Royal and rue St-Denis.

Finish: St-Louis Square.

Time: 2 hours; you may want to take "Walking Tour 10—Ethnic Montréal" afterward.

Metro: Mont-Royal.

Best Time: Monday through Saturday during the day, when the shops are open. Start in the morning or early afternoon if you want to combine the tour with "Walking Tour 10—Ethnic Montréal" or an exploration of Mont-Royal.

Worst Time: Sunday and evenings, when shops are closed, but if you mainly want to café-hop, evenings are fine, too.

Plateau Mont-Royal may be the part of Montréal where Montréalers feel most at home—away from the busy rhythm of downtown and the heavy foot traffic of Old Montréal. North of downtown and due east of Mont-Royal Park, this area has a lively mix of people and an abundance of shops and restaurants. It encompasses pretty Parc Lafontaine, St-Louis Square, and tidy residential streets lined with row houses that are home to students, young professionals, and Portuguese, Greek, and Vietnamese immigrants. Mont-Royal Park is within walking distance of the Plateau, the name "plateau" itself refering to the shoulder of the mountain.

If you like to see where and how people in a city actually live, and get an idea of the tempo of their everyday lives, this is a good tour to take. You won't pass any museums or other "attractions" along the way: This is, plain and simple, a "browsing and grazing" tour.

Start from the Mont-Royal metro station. There's a fruit stand out front and a grocery store as well, so fill up your day pack if you've brought it along. Turn left on avenue du Mont-Royal.

To see the creations of some of Montréal's up-and-coming young designers, cross rue St-Denis and pay a quick visit to:

1. **Barbeau Montréal,** a boutique at 365 avenue du Mont-Royal est carrying fashions in linen, silk, wool, and cotton, as well as hats and children's clothing. All of it's done with creative flair and is best suited to slim figures and full budgets.

    Return to rue St-Denis and turn right onto it. St-Denis is a wonderful street, filled with many places to discover. I've hit some high spots here, but left plenty of room for you to happen upon your own special places.

    In the block between avenue du Mont-Royal and rue Marie-Anne, there's much to explore. On the lefthand side of the street, for instance, is:

2. **Quai de Brumes,** 4481 rue St-Denis, a popular gathering spot for jazz, blues, and beer. A friend described the crowd to me once as "a fairly uniform group of post-'60s francophone smokers." The name Quai de Brumes means "Foggy Dock." Nearby is:

3. **Tintin,** 4419 rue St-Denis, filled with memorabilia related to the popular Belgian cartoon character from whom the shop takes its name.

    Across the street is:

MICHEL TREMBLAY

Born in 1942, the author Michel Tremblay lives in Plateau Montréal and writes about it, too. The second volume of his *Chroniques du Plateau Mont-Royal,* called *Thérèse et Pierrette à l'école des Sainte-Anges,* is set in the Plateau and brings it vividly to life. If you're taken with this part of Montréal, pick up a copy and delve more deeply.

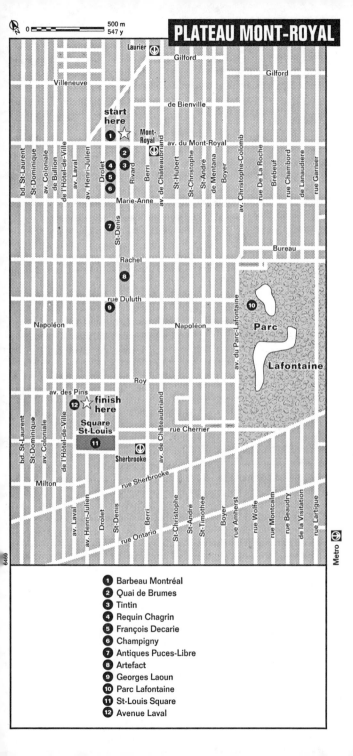

PLATEAU MONT-ROYAL

0 — 500 m / 547 y

Laurier
Gilford
Gilford
Villeneuve
de Bienville
start here
Mont-Royal
av. du Mont-Royal
Marie-Anne
Bureau
Rachel
rue Duluth
Napoléon
Napoléon
Parc Lafontaine
Roy
av. des Pins
finish here
Square St-Louis
rue Cherrier
Sherbrooke
rue Sherbrooke
Milton
rue Ontario

bd. St-Laurent
St-Dominique
av. Coloniale
de Bullion
de l'Hôtel-de-Ville
av. Laval
av. Henri-Julien
Drolet
Rivard
Berri
av. de Châteaubriand
St-Hubert
St-Christophe
St-André
de Mentana
Boyer
av. Christophe-Colomb
rue De La Roche
Brébeuf
rue Chambord
de Lanaudière
rue Garnier
av. du Parc-Lafontaine
St-Denis
rue Christophe
St-André
St-Timothée
Boyer
rue Amherst
rue Wolfe
rue Montcalm
rue Beaudry
de la Visitation
rue Lartigue

Metro

1 Barbeau Montréal
2 Quai de Brumes
3 Tintin
4 Requin Chagrin
5 François Decarie
6 Champigny
7 Antiques Puces-Libre
8 Artefact
9 Georges Laoun
10 Parc Lafontaine
11 St-Louis Square
12 Avenue Laval

6460

4. **Requin Chagrin,** 4430 rue St-Denis, a retro shop with a good selection of secondhand garb, from ties to tweeds, for men and women. Beside it is:

5. **François Decarie,** at 4424 rue St-Denis. This designer creates memorable hats and berets. If you collect either, be sure to take home one of these collectors items. Monsieur Decarie often works in the back of the shop.

   At 4380 rue St-Denis is:

6. **Champigny,** an enormous, well-stocked French bookstore where books are given rooms of their own according to subject matter. It's worth a browse whether you read French or not, and you can certainly find travel books in English, as well as magazines and newspapers from all over the world: the *Washington Post, Wall Street Journal, The European, New York Times,* and the *Village Voice,* to name a few.

   Cross rue Marie-Anne. On the lefthand corner, at 4349 rue St-Denis, is a showroom called Mobilier Interversion—Creations Québécois, which displays and sells modern Québécois furniture. In the middle of the block, at 4279 rue St-Denis, the two-story Ma Maison sells household items from around the world; it is frequented by folks who live in the neighborhood and come here to stock their apartments.

   On the righthand side of rue St-Denis, look for a wonderfully cluttered shop called:

7. **Antiques Puces-Libre,** 4240 rue St-Denis, with three floors of 19th-century French-Canadian country collectibles—pine and oak furniture, lamps, clocks, vases, and much more.

REFUELING STOP Fondumentale, at 4325 rue St-Denis, specializes in—what else—fondue. The turn-of-the-century house and the garden in back are delightful. **Olive,** at 4275 rue St-Denis, is a pleasant Lebanese restaurant.

Continue your stroll down rue St-Denis and cross rue Rachel. On the lefthand side of the street is the Continental Bistro Américain (4169 rue St-Denis), a bar/restaurant that isn't American at all. It's filled with French flair and often has music. Do sneak a peek inside at the striking decor. Close by, you'll spot:

8. **Artefact,** 4117 rue St-Denis, with clothing and paintings by up-and-coming Québécois designers and artists.

   On the opposite side of the street, at the corner of rue Duluth and rue St-Denis, is a large shop for glasses or contact lenses:

9. Georges Laoun, 4012 rue St-Denis. The shop, named after the owner/optician, carries imaginative frames, from the fashionable to the funky. They range in price from $160 to $2,000, but there's no charge to look.

REFUELING STOP L'Express, 3927 rue St-Denis, is a perennially packed French-style bistro that attracts artists, actors, and writers, among others (it's a favorite of mine). You can eat at the counter or at the tables in front or in the back (which is slightly more casual). The food's French and tasty.

Chao Phraya, at 4088 St-Denis near Duluth, is a moderately priced Thai restaurant where you can feast on inexpensive vegetable and noodle dishes or spend a little more for shrimp, chicken, crab, beef, and pork dishes.

Cross to the other side of rue St-Denis, take a right, and walk along rue Duluth, one of the city's most colorful ethnic streets (learn more about it in "Walking Tour 10—Ethnic Montréal"), filled with Portuguese, Greek, Italian, Algerian, and Vietnamese restaurants. (If you don't want to explore this street or the next stop, you can continue down rue St-Denis to St-Louis Square, or follow Duluth in the opposite direction to explore Mont-Royal Park.)

If you walk along rue Duluth in an easterly direction for **9** blocks, it will dead-end and deposit you in pretty:

10. Parc Lafontaine. The land the park occupies was originally part of a farm that stretched from rue Lafontaine north to avenue du Mont-Royal. The colonial government bought this piece of land in 1845 to use for military training; the city acquired it in 1888 and created a public park, one of Montréal's most inviting and undiscovered (to out-of-towners, anyway) pockets of green.

When you enter the park, look in front of you and slightly to the left at a terrace with benches overlooking the water. To me, this is the most serene spot in the park, part of a French-style promenade. I highly recommend you pay it a visit. From the terrace, you'll see (and can easily walk to) a statue of poet Félix Leclerc. Born in 1914 on the island of Ile d'Orleans near Québec City, Leclerc was well-known as a poet and singer and became an unofficial ambassador of French-Canadian culture to the world—and most notably to France, where he lived for many years before returning to Québec. He died on Ile d'Orleans in 1988.

Straight ahead of you is the Théatre de Verdure, an open-air theater that presents free dance, music, and theatrical productions from May to August. To the right of the theater is a large body of water; I suggest strolling in a clockwise direction around it, then making your way to the corner of avenue du Parc Lafontaine and rue Cherrier.

Cross the avenue and follow rue Cherrier back (west) to rue St-Denis. (At rue Berri you'll see the sign for the metro you can take when you complete this walk.) Continue one more block past rue St-Denis to:

11. **St-Louis Square.** This public garden framed by Victorian town houses and with a fountain as its centerpiece is one of the city's most picturesque public squares. St-Louis Square was created on the site of a reservoir built in 1849 to provide water to the eastern part of the city. The gray-stone houses surrounding the square were built between 1880 and 1890 for the city's francophone elite. If you arrive here on a summer day, you might get to hear an impromptu concert.

REFUELING STOP Take your pick from two quite different places: **Witloof,** an elegant Belgian restaurant at 3619 rue St-Denis, or the more casual **Café Cherrier,** 3635 rue St-Denis, with its popular terrace. The latter is particularly popular for weekend brunch and is a great choice for a steaming bowl of café-au-lait or hot chocolate anytime.

The western boundary of St-Louis Square is the picturesque:

12. **avenue Laval.** Most notable along Laval is the block between rue Prince-Arthur and avenue des Pins: Filled with turn-of-the-century row houses with gracefully curving exterior iron stairways and colorful roofs, some with wrought-iron trim, this is as lovely a block as any in Montréal.

From here you can pick up "Walking Tour 10—Ethnic Montréal" to explore more of this part of the city. You could also amble farther down rue St-Denis to the colorful Latin Quarter. Or, if you're ready to call it a day, the Sherbrooke metro station is less than half a block away from St-Louis Square.

Ethnic Montréal

Start: St-Louis Square.
Finish: Rue Duluth.
Time: 2 hours.
Metro: Sherbrooke; take the L'ITHO exit.
Best Time: Anytime. This area is lively, fun, and safe, day or night.

You may know something of Montréal's French and English background, and even its Scottish and Irish heritage, but the modern city is filled with an ethnic diversity most people don't realize. There are many Montréalers—22.8% of the population at last count—whose first language is neither French nor English. It might be Greek, or Portuguese, or Vietnamese, or something else. Just take a trip on the metro and you'll quickly see what a melting pot this city is.

It would be impossible to fit into a single walking tour all of Montréal's major ethnic neighborhoods; and getting from one to the other is not especially scenic anyway. (If you'd like to see some of the Asian, Chinese, black, Greek, Jewish, Latin, or Middle Eastern neighborhoods, however, *The Guide to Ethnic Montréal,* by Barry

Lazar and Tamsin Douglas, can provide the walking tours.) But if you simply want to get a sense of the diversity of Montréal's inhabitants, there are several easy-to-get-to streets that are musts to visit—St-Laurent, Prince-Arthur, and Duluth—and they are conveniently parallel or perpendicular to each other.

This tour is purposely short, and can be readily combined with "Walking Tour 9—Plateau Mont-Royal." If you decide to do both tours, start with Plateau Mont-Royal; the Plateau area actually encompasses rues Duluth and Prince-Arthur.

Start this tour from the Sherbrooke metro station. Take the "L'ITHO" (the city's Tourism and Hotel Institute) exit from the metro, turn right at the top of the escalator, then turn left on the street (rue de Malines) to come to:

1. **St-Louis Square.** This public garden is framed by pretty row houses that were erected for upper-middle-class French-speaking Montréalers in the late-19th and early 20th centuries.

   Cross to the south side (actually the southwestern side) of the square. At avenue Laval, between rue-Prince-Arthur and rue des Pins, note the striking architecture that was typical of Montréal at the turn of the century. Cross avenue Laval into one of the city's most colorful ethnic streets:

2. **rue Prince-Arthur,** a lively pedestrian thoroughfare named after Queen Victoria's third son, who was Governor General of Canada from 1911 to 1916. The street is filled primarily with Greek restaurants, most of which add more to the liveliness of the street than to the gastronomic reputation of the city. (The best Greek restaurant is on nearby rue Duluth; see the second "Refueling Stop" below.) Many of the restaurants require that you bring your own booze, readily available from nearby liquor stores. A "photo op" awaits you at 3601 rue Prince-Arthur (at rue Buillon), where you'll see a house with a striking "nouvelle Monet" mural painted on its bricks.

   Continue along rue Prince-Arthur for 4 blocks until you reach:

3. **boulevard St-Laurent,** where you will turn right. Known locally as "the Main" (as in "Main Street"), it was traditionally a beachhead for immigrants in Montréal, and you are sure to notice the ethnic mix along it on your walk.

   While boulevard St-Laurent is not as stylish as many of the city's other streets, it's compelling in its own right and draws local people in search of bargains (much the same as New York City's 14th Street or Lower East Side).

   In recent years, this central avenue has increasingly become an

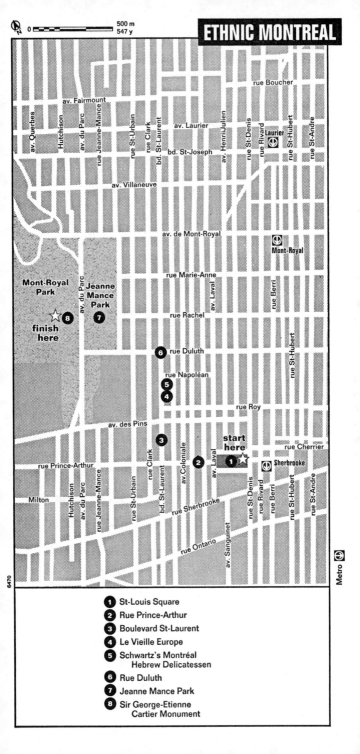

ETHNIC MONTREAL

0   500 m
    547 y

1	St-Louis Square
2	Rue Prince-Arthur
3	Boulevard St-Laurent
4	Le Vieille Europe
5	Schwartz's Montréal Hebrew Delicatessen
6	Rue Duluth
7	Jeanne Mance Park
8	Sir George-Etienne Cartier Monument

avant-garde outpost of chic restaurants and late-night clubs. The stylish late-night section of boulevard St-Laurent runs for several miles, roughly from avenue Viger to avenue Fairmount.

The growth of this trendy bohemian area was fueled in the 1980s by the neighborhood's low rents and the availability of large industrial loft spaces, a legacy of St-Laurent's heyday as a garment manufacturing center. Today, those cavernous spaces have been converted into restaurants and clubs where the area's artistic community and trendsetters hobnob late into the night. Not surprisingly, the rents are not so low anymore.

At 3855 boulevard St-Laurent and rue St-Cuthbert is:

4. La Vieille Europe (Old Europe), a storehouse of culinary sights and smells. It's got cheeses, salamis, sausages, pâtés, nuts, honey, fresh peanut butter, and dried fruits. And you can watch as coffee beans are roasted in the back of the store. From Old Europe to New France, it's quite a treat.

Continue up boulevard St-Laurent; before you reach rue Napoléon, the next cross street, you'll discover one of Montréal's most enduring ethnic outposts:

5. Schwartz's Montréal Hebrew Delicatessen, at 3895 boulevard St-Laurent, open long hours and always crowded. It's not much to look at: a long, narrow space with a lunch counter and a collection of simple tables and chairs crammed together. But nobody comes here for the decor; they line up for the smoked meat served in huge sandwiches.

REFUELING STOP **The Shed Café,** 3515 boulevard St-Laurent, is a popular watering hole and is known for its hefty, tasty desserts. If you're hungry for Italian food, you can go one of two ways: lowbrow (and fun) at **Pizzadelic,** 3509 boulevard St-Laurent, or higher brow at **Buona Notte,** 3528 boulevard St-Laurent.

Four blocks north of rue Prince-Arthur and similar to it is:

6. rue Duluth. The ethnic restaurants here are more diverse, and include Portuguese, Greek, Italian, Algerian, and Vietnamese. They line the street from boulevard St-Laurent to rue St-Hubert, adding color and flavor to the neighborhood.

REFUELING STOP For something a little different, try **Café Berbere,** at 73 rue Duluth, between boulevard

St-Laurent and avenue Coloniale. It serves Algerian and North African fare and is particularly appealing to vegetarians hungry for something other than salad. It's quiet, pleasant, and licensed, and the couscous specialties come highly recommended.

Or do as so many Montréalers do and opt for a Greek meal at **Le Jardin de Panos,** 251 rue Duluth, between Bleury and St-Hubert. Choose from shish kebabs, souvlaki, calimari, Greek salad, moussaka, and beef or seafood brochettes. The bread is memorable and the staff ever efficient—they have to be to handle the crowds they get. Sit on the terrace in summer, and get your wine from the market next door or across the street.

From rue Duluth and boulevard St-Laurent, you have two options. The first is to turn right onto rue Duluth and explore the ethnic-restaurant row as far as rue St-Hubert. Turn right onto St-Hubert and follow it to Cherrier, passing some pretty old houses along the way. At Cherrier, which is near where you started this walking tour, you'll find the Sherbrooke metro stop and nearby, on rue St-Denis, some pleasant cafés.

Your second option is to continue this tour for a few more stops to get a taste of Montréal's green space. If this sounds appealing, turn left and walk three blocks to small:

7. **Jeanne Mance Park,** and through it to avenue du Parc. Cross the avenue at the light to enter the city's well-loved and equally well-used Mont-Royal Park. Just to your right is the:

8. **Sir George-Etienne Cartier Monument,** created by artist George William Hill and unveiled in 1919. On Sundays in warm weather, a cross section of the city's ethnic population gathers around (and on) the monument to listen to drumming. It's all quite impromptu and freewheeling. Nearby, people relax, play with their dogs, or toss Frisbees.

You can explore the park further from here by picking up the wide pedestrian chemin Olmsted, up the hill and to the left of the monument as you face it. You can also explore the park by following "Walking Tour 4—Mont-Royal" at a later time.

REFUELING STOP Founded in 1976, **Santropole,** at 3990 St-Urbain at rue Duluth, near Jeanne-Mance Park, has a long-standing reputation for serving fresh, hefty salads and sandwiches. Even the "small" salads are large, so order accordingly. Besides salads and sandwiches, you can get hot vegetarian pies, fruit, 18 different kinds of milkshakes, and a large variety of herbal teas. One percent of the bill is sent to organizations to ease hunger in Québec and Third World countries. Take-out is available.

SIR GEORGE-ETIENNE CARTIER

Sir George-Etienne Cartier (1814–1873) was an attorney, businessman, and politician who had a long and distinguished career in Canadian government. A Conservative, Cartier was prime minister of Lower Canada (now Québec) in the days before Canadian confederation and promoted the movement for confederation in 1867.

After Canada made its break from Britain and formed its own government, he served as a member of Parliament and as the Minister of Militia (in the latter capacity, he approved the first uniform worn by the Canadian army). Among his accomplishments were the reform of teaching and civil law and the abolition of the seigneurial system in Québec.

Cartier was fond of saying that the secret to Montréal's success was its geographic location, and this has proven true over the years.

The house of this "Father of Confederation," at rue Notre-Dame and rue Berri, is now operated as a museum by the Canadian government.

QUEBEC CITY

Upper Town

Start: Parc des Gouverneurs.
Finish: The Citadel.
Time: 2 hours.
Best Time: Anytime.

Québec City started out at the bottom of a cliff beside the St. Lawrence River, but the fledgling community quickly moved to higher ground to protect itself from attacks by sea, built a fortress, and surrounded itself with a sturdy stone wall. In 1842, Charles Dickens called it "the Gibraltar of America, a place not to be forgotten or mixed up in the mind with other places." In 1907, Rudyard Kipling would add his own testament to the uniqueness of this city that "ranks by herself among the Mother-cities of whom none can say 'This reminds me.'"

Today Québec City is the only walled city in North America north of Mexico, and in December 1985 it became the only city in North America to be honored by UNESCO as a World Heritage City.

It's fitting that a visit to the city start in Québec's Upper Town, still wrapped in its stone wall, peering over the crest of Cap Diamant (Cape Diamond) at the river below. Today the only onslaught the city has to face is the many admirers who come from all over the world to see it.

Begin this tour at:

1. **Parc des Gouverneurs** (Governors' Park), right behind the Château Frontenac. The park takes its name from the site of the mansion that housed the French governors of Québec. It burned in 1834, and whatever ruins there may have been were buried under the great mass of the Château Frontenac when it was built in 1893.

   The obelisk monument in the park is dedicated to *both* generals in the momentous battle of September 13, 1759, when Wolfe (British) and Montcalm (French) fought it out, determining the ultimate destiny of Québec. The British were victorious, but Wolfe, wounded in the fighting, lived only long enough to hear of his victory; Montcalm died after Wolfe, knowing the city was lost.

   In summer the Parc des Gouverneurs is the scene of various shows and musical programs sponsored by the municipal government. Many of the city's fine small hotels are clustered around or near the park.

   The park is actually in two levels. Cannons were set up on the lower level, as they are today (though these are not the original cannons). Beyond it, and you can take the stairs for a closer look, is the inviting:

2. **Terrasse Dufferin** (Dufferin Terrace), the boardwalk-lookout with its perky green-and-white-topped gazebos. It's easy to imagine it as it looked 100 years ago, with ladies with parasols and gentlemen with canes strolling along it on a sunny afternoon, Château Frontenac as a backdrop. Samuel de Champlain, Québec's founder, built Fort St-Louis here in 1620, and died in it in 1635.

   The terrace takes its name from one of the governors of New France, Lord Dufferin, and the boardwalk, a shorter version of the one you see today, was installed in 1838. Follow the terrace down to the right as you face the river and it will lead you to the:

3. **Promenade des Gouverneurs.** Sometime during your visit, follow the promenade, which skirts the sheer cliff wall and takes you past the Citadel and on to Battlefields Park, a 20-minute walk away. (If you take "Walking Tour 12—The Grande Allée and Battlefields Park," you'll walk along the promenade in the reverse—downhill—direction.) For now, return to the southeast corner of the Parc des Gouverneurs where you'll see the:

4. **United States Consulate,** a handsome three-story brick

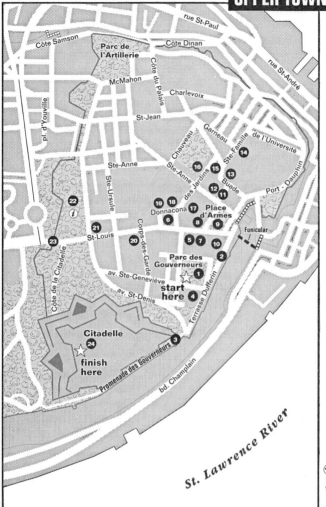

UPPER TOWN

0 —————— 250 m
         278 y

rue St-Paul
Côte Samson
Côte Dinan
rue St-André
Parc de l'Artillerie
McMahon
Côte du Palais
Charlevoix
pl. d'Youville
St-Jean
Ste-Anne
Garneau
Chauveau
Ste-Famille de l'Université
Ste-Anne
des Jardins
14
16
15
13
Buade
Port - Dauphin
22
(i)
Ste-Ursule
12
11
19 **18**
Donnacona
17
Place d'Armes
21
St-Louis
6
8
9
Funicular
23
Côte de la Citadelle
Corps-des-Garde
20
5 **7**
10
2
Parc des Gouverneurs
1
av. Ste-Geneviève
start here
av. St-Denis
4
Terrasse Dufferin
Citadelle
3
24
finish here
Promenade des Gouverneurs
bd. Champlain

St. Lawrence River

Information **(i)**

1 Parc des Gouverneurs
2 Terrasse Dufferin
3 Promenade des Gouverneurs
4 United States Consulate
5 Maison Kent
6 Maison Jacquet
7 Maison Maillou
8 Québec Ministry of Finance
9 Place d'Armes
10 Château Frontenac
11 Rue du Tresor
12 Les Promenades du Vieux Québec
13 Basilica Notre-Dame-de-Québec
14 Québec Seminary
15 Statue of Elzear Alexandre Taschereau
16 Hôtel-de-Ville
17 Holy Trinity Anglican Cathedral
18 Ursuline Museum and Chapel
19 Ursuline Convent
20 Cannonball
21 Manoir d'Esplanade
22 Tourist information office
23 St-Louis Gate
24 Citadelle

6471

building with a copper roof and United States flags out front. American citizens can drop in during the week, except holidays.

From the Parc des Gouverneurs, walk up rue Mont-Carmel, which runs between the park and the Château Frontenac, and turn right onto rue Haldimand. At the next corner, rues Haldimand and St-Louis, stands a white house with blue trim called:

5. **Maison Kent** (Kent House). Built in 1648, it is possibly the oldest building in Québec. Although it is most famous for being the place in which De Ramezay signed the capitulation of Québec to the British forces in 1759, its name comes from the Duke of Kent. The duke, Queen Victoria's father, lived here from 1792 to 1794, just prior to the time that he married Victoria's mother in an arranged liaison. His true love, it is said, had lived with him in the Maison Kent.

Today Maison Kent houses the Consulate General of France, as the tricolor over the door attests. This seems fitting since in 1648, D'Ailleboust, the governor of New France, lived in the house when it was first built.

Cater-corner to Maison Kent, at rue St-Louis and rue des Jardins, is:

6. **Maison Jacquet** (Jacquet House), a small house with a red roof and red trim, dating from 1677. This charming traditional Old Québec dwelling now houses the restaurant Aux Anciens Canadiens, which serves traditional Québécois food. Another of the oldest houses in the province, it has sheltered some prominent Québécois, including Philippe Aubert de Gaspé, the author of *Les Anciens Canadiens,* who lived here from 1815 to 1824. The restaurant takes its name from his book, which recounts the history and folklore of Québec and the Québécois.

REFUELING STOP You can check out Québécois home cooking in **Aux Anciens Canadiens** or go around the corner to **Café de la Paix,** at 44 rue des Jardins, a warm and cozy café that serves outstanding French fare with a flourish.

From Maison Jacquet, walk along quaint but commercial rue St-Louis, past the Maison Kent, to no. 17, the:

7. **Maison Maillou** (Maillou House), a stone house with five dormer windows, three chimneys, and foundations and ground floor dating from 1736. The Québec Military Council met here

from 1760 to 1764. The house was enlarged in 1799, and later restored in 1959. Note the metal shutters used, perhaps, to thwart 18th-century unfriendly fire. Now the building houses the Québec Board of Trade and Industry.

The large building across the street from Maison Maillou is the impressive French Renaissance–style:

8. Québec Ministry of Finance, also known as the old courthouse. It started out in 1799 as a courthouse, was renovated between 1927 and 1934, and was restored again from 1983 to 1987. Since 1987 it has been Québec's Ministry of Justice, the name on the facade notwithstanding.

The architect for the building's exterior was Eugene-Etienne Tache, Minister of Public Works at that time. (Another Monsieur Tache, Etienne Pascal, a former prime minister of Canada, would be responsible for the plans for Québec City's Parliament Building almost 100 years later.) The interior of the building is art deco. The street fronting the Ministry of Finance building is a popular parking spot for calèches, the horse-drawn carriages that tour the city.

Continue down rue St-Louis to arrive at:

9. place d'Armes, once the military parade ground in front of the governors' mansion (which no longer exists). In the small park at the center of the square is the *Monument to the Faith,* which recalls the arrival of Recollets monks from France in 1615. The Recollets were granted a large plot of land by the king of France in 1681 for their church and monastery; today the land is occupied by the Ministry of Finance and the Anglican Church.

Facing the square is the monument to Samuel de Champlain, who founded Québec in 1608. Created by French artists Paul Chevre and Paul le Cardonel, the statue has stood here since 1898. The stone that the statue's pedestal is made from is the same as that used in Paris's Arc de Triomphe and Sacré-Coeur Basilica.

Near the Champlain monument is the striking diamond-shaped monument designating Québec City a UNESCO World Heritage Site, the only city in North America to be so honored. Erected here in 1985, it is made of bronze, granite, and glass: The outside circle represents the world; the square, the achievements of human beings; and the prism at its core, a world heritage treasure. A tourist information center is also at place d'Armes, at 12 rue Ste-Anne.

By now you've seen almost every angle of the bewitching:

10. Château Frontenac, Québec skyline's literal and architectural high point. The château was built as a hotel in 1892–93 by the Canadian Pacific Railway Company, which still owns it today. The architect, Bruce Price of New York, raised his creation on the site of the governor's mansion and named it after Louis de Buade, Comte de Frontenac. Monsieur le Comte was the one who, in 1690, was faced with the threat of an English fleet under Sir William Phips. Phips sent a messenger to demand Frontenac's surrender, but Frontenac replied, "Tell your lord that I will reply with the mouths of my cannons." Which he did. Phips sailed away. A tour guide once described Frontenac to me, to my glee, as a "dreadful, irascible old warrior."

REFUELING STOP This is a great part of town just to sit and watch the world drift by. Grab a sidewalk table and enjoy something to drink at **Au Café Suisse,** 26 rue Ste-Anne, or a bite to eat at **Au Relais de la place d'Armes,** 16 rue Ste-Anne. There's also a convenient short-order café on the ground level of the Château Frontenac, with an entrance near the monument to Champlain.

From the château, cross St-Louis and walk back through place d'Armes to rue Ste-Anne. Perpendicular to Ste-Anne is a narrow, pedestrian street called:

11. **rue du Tresor,** where artists hang their paintings and illustrations. It is reliably lively with buyers and sellers, and prices are kept within the means of the average visitor. Several of the artists, strategically positioned near the sidewalk cafés, draw portraits or caricatures, and they can chalk you onto a large piece of paper in no time at all.

In the middle of rue du Tresor, set back from the street, is:

12. **Les Promenades du Vieux Québec,** a modern building filled with upscale boutiques and galleries and a theater presenting the 3-D "Québec Experience" about the city's history. Don those 3-D glasses and go back in time.

Follow rue du Tresor to rue Buade and turn left. At the corner of rue Ste-Famille, on your right, is the:

13. **Basilica Notre-Dame-de-Québec** (1647), which has seen a tumultuous history of bombardment, reconstruction, and restoration. Its interior is ornate, the air rich with the scent of burning candles. Many valuable old paintings and ecclesiastical treasures remain from the time of the French regime. The chancel lamp was a gift from Louis XIV.

The crypt is the final resting place for most of the bishops of

Québec. The rooster is atop the basilica for religious, not agricultural, reasons (remember St. Peter?), though the first settlers here were farmers. (A fine statue dedicated to Québec's first farmer, Louis Hebert, was moved from near here to Parc Montmorency.)

Continue downhill from the basilica on rue Ste-Famille. Just past Côte de la Fabrique is the historic:

14. **Québec Seminary,** founded in 1663 by Bishop Laval, the first bishop in North America. The seminary had grown into Laval University by 1852, and for many years it occupied the much-expanded seminary campus. By the middle of the 20th century, however, it had outgrown its campus, and a new, modern university was constructed west of the city in Ste-Foy. No matter—the entire area is still known as the Latin Quarter after the language that once dominated university life. You may want to return later (it's lively at night) to see more of this area, including rues Couillard, Garneau, and St-Jean.

During summer only, tours of the old seminary's quiet grounds and some of its stone and wood buildings are given, revealing a lavish use of stone, tile, and brass, and great gilt-framed oil paintings, all symbols of the church's power and influence at one time. Inside the seminary's museum, at 9 rue de l'Université, is a scale model of the seminary which gives an idea of its size and layout.

From here, head back to the basilica, take a right on rue Buade, and follow it to rue des Jardins. At the corner of place de l'Hôtel-de-Ville, you'll see a:

15. **statue of Elzear Alexandre Taschereau** pointing to the basilica. Cardinal Taschereau, Canada's first cardinal, was appointed in 1866, the first of an unbroken succession of cardinals from Québec City until 1953, when the bishop of Montréal was named cardinal. Taschereau was also a founder of Laval University and he worked with typhoid victims quarantined on Grosse Ile, near Montmagny, in 1847.

Facing his statue is the:

16. **Hôtel-de-Ville** (City Hall), built in 1883. The building's lower level, with an entrance on Côte de la Fabrique, houses the Centre d'Interpretation (Urban Life Interpretation Center), with a large scale model of part of Québec City and its suburbs as they were in 1975. It'll help you get your bearings, and you might be surprised to see how spread-out the city actually is: Although the Old Town is very compact, the city actually covers 35½ square miles (92 square kilometers).

City Hall Park was designed for easy conversion into an

outdoor arena, and in summer—especially during the Festival d'Été International (Québec International Summer Festival)—concerts, dance shows, and other programs are staged here.

Continue on rue des Jardins and cross rue Ste-Anne. To your left you'll see the spire of the:

17. Holy Trinity Anglican Cathedral, which dates from 1804. If it looks vaguely familiar, that's because it was modeled after Saint-Martin-in-the-Fields in London. The interior of the handsome cathedral is simple but spacious, with pews of solid English oak from the Royal Windsor Forest and a latticed ceiling in white with a gilded-chain motif. England's King George III donated some of the objects on view in the cathedral, which was renovated in 1992. If you visit the church, you may happen upon an organ recital or the rehearsal for one.

Farther along on rue des Jardins, at 12 rue Donnacona, on the right side of the street, is the:

18. Ursuline Museum and Chapel. The museum displays the handiwork of the Ursuline nuns from the 17th, 18th, and 19th centuries. You'll also see Amerindian crafts and the cape made from the bedroom drapes of Anne of Austria and given to Marie de l'Incarnation, the reverend mother and a founder of the convent, when she left France for New France in 1639.

Be sure to peek into the restored chapel if it's open. The chapel shelters the remains of General Montcalm, who was buried here after he fell in the battle that marked the end of French rule in Québec in 1759. Montcalm's tomb is actually under the chapel and not accessible to the public; his skull, on the other hand, is on display in the Ursuline Museum. (This seems disrespectful to me, but I'm sure they have their reasons.) You can, however, see the tomb of Marie de l'Incarnation (it is to the right) and the altar, created by sculptor Pierre-Noel Levasseur between 1726 and 1736 and considered a masterpiece of Canadian wood sculpture.

From the museum, turn right on rue Donnacona and walk a short block to the gate entry of the:

19. Ursuline Convent, built originally in 1642 as a girls' school. What you see of the convent today is actually a succession of different buildings added and repaired at various times up to 1836 (fires were frequent, and took their toll on the buildings). A statue of founder Marie de l'Incarnation is outside.

The convent is a private girls school today and is not open to the public. If you could go inside, you would see, in the older part, some timberwork and a wooden staircase considered the finest example of 17th-century architecture still in Canada.

Continue up the hill along rue Donnacona to rue St-Louis;

MARIE DE L'INCARNATION

The founder of the Ursuline teaching order in Québec, Marie Guyart was born in Tours in 1599. At age 18, she married Claude Martin, had a son, and was widowed two years later. In 1631, at the age of 32, she entered the Ursuline order, and eight years later left France for a three-month voyage that would bring her to Québec.

Her convent started out on place Royale in the Lower Town, but by 1642 it had moved to the Upper Town to the location that is still its home. Her goal was to educate Amerindian and French girls. She respected the culture of the native peoples and learned the Montagnais, Algonquin, Iroquois, and Huron languages, so that she could communicate.

Marie de l'Incarnation has been called the Mother of New France, and for over 350 years the Ursulines have continued her work of education in Canada. On June 22, 1980, she was declared *bienheureuse,* or blessed, by Pope John Paul II.

cross the street and turn right. At the next block, at rue du Corps-de-Garde, note the:

20. cannonball lodged at the base of the tree trunk. It purportedly landed here during the War of 1759 and over the years has become inseparable from the tree.

   Continue along St-Louis another block and a half to rue d'Auteuil. Consider the house on the corner, on your right, now a small hotel called:

21. Manoir d'Esplanade. Notice that many of the windows in the facade facing rue St-Louis are bricked up. This is because houses were once taxed by the number of windows they had, and the frugal homeowner found a way to get around the law; it cut down on his view, but shored up his budget.

   If you need a map, some brochures, or a rest room, turn right on rue d'Auteuil and walk to the:

22. tourist information office, set in Parc de l'Esplanade, nestled just inside the city walls. The eternal unmelting snowman out front is Bonhomme Carnaval, mascot of the city's Winter Carnival (more about him in "Walking Tour 12—The Grande Allée and Battlefields Park"). Before it became a public space, Parc de l'Esplanade was a military exercise ground.

THE REGIMENTAL GOAT

In 1844 Queen Victoria was given a goat from the Shah of Persia, marking the beginning of the royal herd. More than 100 years later, in 1955, Queen Elizabeth presented a goat from the royal herd to Canada's 22nd Regiment. The goat, named Batisse, and his descendents—all named either Batisse or Catherine—have participated in the special events, parades, and ceremonies of the regiment.

Queen Elizabeth's gift was not so peculiar. The idea of a regimental goat in the British Army goes back to the Welsh Fusiliers, who brought their goat with them to Bunker Hill during the War of Independence.

When at leisure, the regimental goat and his family live a secluded life at the Québec Zoo, not unlike their royal kin in England, who reside at the London Zoo.

REFUELING STOP   Apsara, at 71 rue d'Auteuil, is a pretty Indonesian restaurant in a fine old town house that is now an inn. The menu features many Thai temptations, such as beef with spices and breaded shrimp in a spicy sauce.

Walk back to rue St-Louis, cross it, and turn right. In front of you looms the:

23. St-Louis Gate, constructed by the English in 1873 on the site of a gate built by the French in 1692. It is one of four gates in the 2.8-mile (4.6-kilometer) fortified wall encircling the city, and was designed from a plan drawn up by Québec architect Charles Baillairgé; Baillairgé also designed the old prison, now part of the Québec Museum. Beyond St-Louis Gate, the street broadens to become the Grande Allée, where "Walking Tour 12—The Grande Allée and Battlefields Park" begins.

Before you reach the gate, however, turn left onto the somewhat forbidding road (Côte de la Citadelle) that leads to an even more forbidding place, the:

24. Citadelle. As you follow the walkway to the Citadelle, take a moment to notice the large stone to the right. It rests on the remains of 13 men who fought and fell in battle with American General Richard Montgomery on New Year's Eve 1775 (the day before many of the American mercenaries' contracts were due to expire), in a joint attack against Québec City with General

Benedict Arnold. Montgomery's remains were moved to St. Paul's Church in New York City in 1818; during his military career, he fought in the French and Indian War, in the American Revolutionary War, and at Louisbourg (Cape Breton Island), Ticonderoga, Montréal, and Martinique and Havana.

The Citadelle, a great star-shaped fortress (the largest in North America), keeps watch from a grassy 37-acre plateau 360 feet (109 meters) above the banks of the St. Lawrence River. Construction by the English, using a French plan, began in 1820 (a decision taken after the city had withstood attacks from the Americans from 1775 through 1812) and took 30 years to complete, by which time it had become obsolete.

Since 1920, the Citadelle has been the home of Canada's Royal 22nd Regiment, which fought in both world wars and in the Korean War. It is the country's only regiment that receives its orders only in French, and its presence here makes the Citadelle the largest fortified group of buildings still occupied by troops in North America.

You can explore the Citadelle and its two military museums only as part of an hour-long tour (tours in English begin every 15 minutes before and after the hour, from 9am to 4pm daily). A summer visit might coincide with the changing of the guard or the beating-the-retreat ceremony, weather permitting.

The Grande Allée & Battlefields Park

Start: The Grande Allée at St-Louis Gate.
Finish: Terrasse Dufferin.
Time: 2½ to 3 hours.
Best Time: Morning to mid-afternoon, to allow plenty of time to explore the park during the day.

The Grande Allée, Québec City's impressive boulevard that begins just outside St-Louis Gate, is the address for the city's stately Parliament Building, in front of which the Winter Carnival takes place every year (the ice sculptures pop up across the street); numerous outdoor cafés and fine restaurants; two popular discos; and the Québec Museum. Just off it lies Battlefields Park and the legendary Plains of Abraham, where Québec's history springs dramatically to life. Most of city's largest hotels are on or near the Grand Allée, and avenue Cartier, which is perpendicular to it and near the museum, is another popular café street.

Start this tour just outside the city wall and St-Louis Gate at the:

1. Grande Allée, the finest thoroughfare in the city. Once a

Map labels:

- rue Crémazie
- bd. René-Lévesque
- Parc de l'Améri Française
- St-Amable
- av. Bourlamaque
- av. Cartier
- av. de Salaberry
- av. Turnbull
- des Érables
- Grande-Allée
- av. Galipeault
- av. Laurier
- av. Taché
- place Montcalm
- Municipal Playground
- av. Wolfe-Montcalm
- Wolfe's Well
- av. Briand
- de Bernières
- Wolfe Monument
- av. George VI
- av. Garneau
- Battlefields Park
- av. Ontario
- av. Ontario
- rue Champlain
- bd. Champlain

St. Lawrenc

1. Grande Allée
2. Site of Winter Carnival
3. Parliament Building
4. Pigeonier
5. Marie Guyart Building
6. Military Drill Hall
7. Jardin Jeanne d'Arc
8. Martello Tower no. 2
9. Rotary
10. Québec Museum
11. Baillairgé Pavilion
12. Maison Henry-Stuart
13. Avenue Cartier
14. Battlefields Park

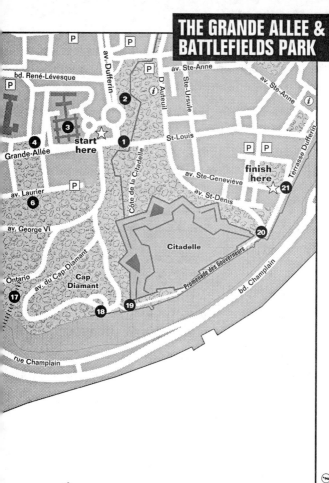

THE GRANDE ALLÉE & BATTLEFIELDS PARK

bd. René-Lévesque

av. Dufferin

av. Ste-Anne

av. Ste-Anne

D'Auteuil

Ste-Ursule

Grande-Allée

start here

St-Louis

Terrasse Dufferin

av. Laurier

av. Ste-Geneviève

finish here

av. St-Denis

av. George VI

Citadelle

Ontario

av. du Cap-Diamant

Cap Diamant

Promenade des Gouverneurs

bd. Champlain

rue Champlain

River

Parking P Information *i*

15 Fountain, sundial, and kiosk
16 Martello Tower no. 1
17 Grand Champlain Stairs
18 Scenic lookout
19 Promenade des Gouverneurs
20 Toboggan ramp
21 Terrasse Dufferin

simple tree-lined road outside the city walls, it took on a new personality with the construction of the stately Parliament Building in 1884. After that, an address on the Grande Allée was coveted.

But there was an earlier time when walking along the Grande Allée was not unlike walking the plank: In the 17th century, those sentenced to death by hanging walked along the Grande Allée to meet the hangman. Today those walking along it are usually in search of lodging, a good meal, or a hot dance floor. They're sure to find all three.

As you gaze up the Grande Allée (with your back to the gate), to your right is a park that runs alongside the city walls. This is the:

2. **Site of Winter Carnival,** one of the most captivating events in North America. The 11-day celebration takes place every year from the first Thursday to the second Sunday of February. A majestic palace of snow and ice, the centerpiece of the festivities, rises dramatically on this spot. Colorfully clad Québécois come to admire it, climb on it, and sample some maple syrup candy at the nearby sugar shack set up for the occasion. The maple syrup is poured on ice and then rolled onto a popsicle stick (you get to roll your own), resulting in a sweet treat.

Across the street, larger-than-life ice sculptures are created by 20 teams of artists from around the world participating in the International Snow Sculpture Competition; each sculpture illustrates some aspect of the culture of the country it represents.

Fronting the park, on avenue Dufferin, stands Québec's stately:

3. **Parliament Building** (Hôtel du Parlement), constructed in 1884. Along the facade are 22 bronze statues of the most illustrious figures in Québec's colorful and tumultuous history. The fountain in front, the work of Philippe Hébert (1890), was dedicated to Québec's original Native American, or Amerindian, inhabitants. You can tour the gilded and sumptuous rooms inside, where symbols of the fleur-de-lys, the initials "VR" (for Victoria Regina), and the maple leaf are constant reminders of Québec's multinational heritage. If the crown on top of the building is lit, Parliament is in session.

Continuing up the hill, on the same side of the street as the Parliament Building, you'll come to a small park where free outdoor concerts are performed in July during the Festival d'été International (Québec International Summer Festival), the largest French-speaking cultural event in North America. Other than that, no activities go on here, except at the well-used:

BONHOMME CARNAVAL

The official mascot of Winter Carnival, Bonhomme looks a bit like the Pillsbury doughboy made of snow. He makes his home at the ice palace but puts in lots of public appearances all over the city during the festival; he gets to crown the queen, lead parades, and thrill children.

At the closing ceremonies of the carnival, Bonhomme bids one and all a fond farewell until the next year, yet the affable snowman has been known to show up at special occasions during the year, especially when they benefit some of his favorite people, children and the elderly.

Bonhomme is a clean-living fellow who probably drinks nothing stronger than milk, certainly not the hard stuff called "caribou" that flows freely during Winter Carnival.

4. Pigeonier, in the righthand corner of the park. It's essentially a condo for pigeons. Soft-hearted Québécois hated the fact that the birds suffered during the province's cold winters so they rigged up this oversized, heated birdhouse—which the pigeons put to good use.

The tall building behind the park and the Pigeonier (in fact, the tallest building around) with an antenna on top is the:

5. Marie Guyart Building, named after Marie de l'Incarnation (Guyart was her secular name), founder of the Ursuline convent and school in Québec in 1639. On the building's 31st floor is an observation deck, called Anima G, the highest lookout point in the city. Anima G is open to the public weekdays from 10am to 4pm and on Saturday, Sunday, and holidays from 1pm to 5pm. Best of all: It's free to the public, and the view is spectacular.

On the opposite side of the Grande Allée from the Marie Guyart Building and the Piggeonier is place Georges V and the:

6. Military Drill Hall, a striking building constructed in 1885 with wrought-iron trim running the width of its roof. The hall inside measures 90 by 260 feet (30 by 80 meters) and is not supported by columns but by the stone walls of the building. The building's architect, Eugene-Etienne Tache, also designed Québec's old courthouse, now the Ministry of Justice, on place d'Armes. The Drill Hall is still used for military purposes, especially drilling for cadets and the army reserve corps.

REFUELING STOP Continue along the Grande-Allée 1 block to rue d'Artigny and the famous strip of cafés that gives the boulevard its nickname "The Champs-Elysée of Québec City." If you only want a drink or light fare, mainly crêpes, choose **Au Petit Coin Breton,** on the south side of the street at 655 Grande Allée est. If serious French fare (and a heftier check) suits you better, then choose **Restaurant Louis Hébert,** on the north side of the street at 688 Grande-Allée est.

Follow the Grande-Allée past place Georges V to place Montcalm; turn left, passing Loew's Le Concorde Hotel, and walk into the:

7. **Jardin Jeanne d'Arc** (Joan of Arc Garden), an oasis of color and tranquility that has been here since 1938. It is filled with more than 100 species of flowers, half of them annuals, in bloom from April to October. The statue of Joan of Arc on horseback, sword held high, that dominates the French garden was a gift to Québec City from an admiring American couple who chose to remain anonymous. If I lived in Québec City, this would be my chosen "thinking spot," a place to come and contemplate life, or to escape from it for a while.

At the far end of the garden, at avenue Laurier and avenue Taché, to your right you'll see the round, stone:

8. **Martello Tower no. 2.** Another one, Tower no. 1, is visible from here, off to the left. These are two of sixteen such structures built in eastern Canada as defense posts against the young upstart nation to the south, in case it took a notion to try and annex its northern neighbor.

The Québec City towers were built between 1808 and 1812 in a straight line from a cliff overlooking the St. Lawrence River inland to Ste-Genevieve Hill, and they are known as towers 1, 2, 3, and 4. It is believed that all four were once connected by underground passageways. The towers were manned by the British army until 1846. When the army left for England in 1871, the towers were turned over to the Canadian government. From 1902 to 1936, one of the towers served as the water tower for the Ross Rifle Factory, which was on the Plains of Abraham. From 1941 to 1962, this same tower was used as an observatory by the Royal Astronomical Society of Canada. Three of the towers are still standing—the one in the park, the one across the street from Jardin Jeanne d'Arc, and the one on Ste-Genevieve Hill.

The National Battlefields Commission acquired one tower in

1910 and the other two in 1936 (the fourth was demolished in 1905) and has restored all three. The tower in the park, Tower no. 1, and the one across from Jardin Jeanne d'Arc, Tower no. 2, are open to the public in summer only. The latter has exhibits on astronomy and its place in the park's history.

Continue your tour by picking up the walkway just to the right of avenue Georges VI, which passes a marker where General Wolfe fell in battle and leads you to a:

9. Rotary. The monument at the center of it was dedicated by the British Army in Canada in 1849. The road leading to it from the Grande Allée is called avenue Wolfe-Montcalm. Off it, to your right as you face the Grande Allée, you'll see the well where water was drawn for the dying General Wolfe.

The rotary is directly in front of the:

10. Québec Museum, at 1 avenue Wolfe-Montcalm. The museum, which opened in 1933, houses the largest collection of Québec art in North America, eight galleries' worth, spanning

MARTELLO TOWERS

Martello Towers were typical of military engineering from 1800 to 1832, particularly in England and Ireland. Because of their simple architecture, they were inexpensive to build. A thick (16.4 feet) western wall was four times thicker than the eastern wall because it was exposed to attack. In the event the enemy took over the tower, it could be blasted from the east with cannons.

Québec City's towers, depending on their size, held 12 or 20 soldiers. The men stayed for a month at a time, except in winter, when the towers stood empty. The only entrances to the towers were on the second floor, facing east. Once all the men were inside, they pulled the moveable stairs in after them. Openings in the wall provided ventilation and outlets for guns. The flooring was wood, probably oak, and hanging oil lamps provided light. The men slept in two-tiered berths against the heftier western wall. There were no latrines, so they made do with chamber pots. Cooking was done in a big pot hanging in the fireplace.

For defense purposes, 16 Martello Towers were built in Canada to ward off attacks from the Americans: four in Québec City, five in Halifax, one in Saint John, New Brunswick, and six in Kingston, Ontario.

the time from the beginning of the colony to the present. In 1992 the museum doubled its exhibition space by incorporating an existing neighboring building, now known as the:

11. **Baillairgé Pavilion.** It actually was the city's old prison, designed in 1867 by one of the city's most esteemed architects, Charles Baillairgé, to house 250 male and female inmates. Later, it became a youth hostel, nicknamed "La Petite Bastille."

The pavilion houses six galleries of temporary exhibits. A cellblock has been left intact as an exhibit in and of itself, and the tower—which you shouldn't miss for the art or the view—contains a provocative sculpture called *Le Plongeur* (*The Diver*) by David Moore, an Irish artist who lives in Montréal.

A modern entry with a needle-nose roof joins the two museum buildings; designed by Charles Dorval and Louis Fortin, it houses the reception area, a stylish café, and a museum shop. The museum is free on Wednesday; there is an admission fee on other days.

The Park Interpretation Center is in the Baillairgé Pavilion on the ground floor. To get to it, turn left after you enter the museum, or you can enter from the parking-lot side of the Baillairgé Pavilion. The large sculpture at the entrance to the Interpretation Center, *Le Parc* by Aline Martineau, depicts the park and those who have known it over the years—Amerindians, immigrants, soldiers, picnickers, soccer players, and kite flyers.

If you have time, invest 25 minutes to explore the center's audiovisual maze, which relates the history of the park in a most lively way. Pick up a park map while you're here.

REFUELING STOP Take a break at the **museum café,** near the information desk at the museum entry. You can get a quick cup of tea or coffee or indulge in a meal before continuing on your walk.

From the museum, you have two choices: Either go directly into the park (pick this tour up again at stop 14), or take about 15 minutes to explore a part of Québec City that many visitors overlook because they never realize it's there.

To do this bit of extra exploring, return to the Grande Allée via avenue Wolfe-Montcalm, turn right on Grande Allée and walk 1 block to the corner of avenue Cartier, where you'll see the:

12. Maison Henry-Stuart, 1195 avenue Cartier, with an entrance on the Grande Allée opposite avenue Briand. The striking yellow brick house with a wraparound porch and central chimney sits in a tree-filled yard framed by a green picket fence. With its green shutters and sloping tin roof, it looks like it might be more at home in Key West than Québec City.

The house was built for a wealthy English merchant, and its ground floor is filled with objects typical of English bourgeois life in Québec City at the turn of the century. (The Québec Council for Monuments and Sites has an office on the second floor.) Small groups (but not individuals, as of this writing) may tour the first floor on Thursday or Sunday by reservation for a fee.

From here, stroll down:

13. avenue Cartier, noted for its stretch of restaurants and cafés from the Grande Allée to rue Crémazie. The avenue is better known to local folks than to visitors because it's a bit removed from the city's major tourist haunts—which is exactly its appeal. At place Quartier Cartier, on avenue Cartier and rue Saunders, you'll find shops, a bakery, and food market.

REFUELING STOP Do as the locals do and drop by **La Brûlerie Rousseau,** located on the ground level of place Quartier Cartier, for a cup or bowl of coffee or hot chocolate. Rest rooms are on the lower level (down the stairs beside the elevator at the main entrance).

Make your way back to the park via avenue Wolfe-Montcalm. Go around the righthand side of the Québec Museum and then to the back of it; you'll pass a playing field to your right. Once you've done this, consider yourself in the thick of:

14. Battlefields Park (Parc des Champs-de-Bataille), also known as the Plains of Abraham. This well-loved and much-used city park has an abundance of historical significance. The park takes its name from Abraham Martin, a Scottish farmer who arrived in Québec in 1617. A few years later, he made his home on the plains above the city, and the area quickly became known as "Abraham." His original acres are all part of the present park, though in 1760 the park was two times its present size; as the city expanded, the park acreage shrank.

It was on this land that the Battle of Québec took place in

1759; it was a short, bloody encounter with the British and French facing off only 40 yards apart. One line of defense advanced, was shot down, and another took its place. The entire battle lasted less than half an hour, and the generals on both sides, Montcalm and Wolfe, died. The battle put an end to New France, though not to the French spirit, which had already put down deep roots in Québec soil and in the hearts of its people.

Battles weren't the only cause of death on the Plains of Abraham. In 1763, Marie-Josephte Corriveau, known as "La Corriveau," was marched up the Grande Allée and hung here, near where Loew's Le Concorde Hotel is today, for killing her second husband. (Rumor has it that she had killed the first one as well.) Her body was suspended in an iron cage to discourage similar behavior from other wives; many years later, the cage became part of Phineas Barnum's famous traveling circus.

By the end of the 18th century, this blood-soaked land was used for happier purposes. The military used the area for recreation, and by the middle of the 19th century civilians joined them. Horse-racing events took place here from the 1760s into the 1900s. The grassy fields also were the scene for cricket matches, lacrosse, tobogganing, and snowshoeing.

In 1874 an observatory for meteorology and astronomy was built here, and in 1897 Buffalo Bill and his Wild West Show wowed crowds in the park, in front of what today is the Québec Museum. In April 1928, about a year after his solo flight across the Atlantic, Lucky Lindy (Charles Lindbergh) touched down here briefly.

In 1908, the National Battlefields Commission was created to preserve the site. Landscape architect Frederick Todd was commissioned to design the park, about which he wrote: "Nothing can prevent the magnificent views obtainable from these plains from being the great characteristic feature of the park, but the whole park is so bound up in the history of this continent that the opportunity of designing the park in such a way as to perpetuate this history would seem to be much more interesting than to lay it out as an ordinary park, with clumps of trees dotted about, and the whole cut up with walks and drives."

Today the park covers 266 acres (107 hectares) and contains almost 5,000 trees representing more than 80 species; prominent among them are sugar maple, silver maple, Norway maple, American elm, and American ash and hawthorn. Mosaic planting, where plants are used to create a design or words, has been utilized throughout the park since 1910.

In summer, if you need a respite from walking, a shuttle bus will spin you through the park in its entirety in about 20 minutes. There's a small fee.

Walk down the hill behind the museum to rue Ontario, cross it, and turn left onto the walking trail that hugs the road. If you prefer, you can soon pick up the one that goes through the woods and is closer to the cliff's edge. Expect to be on this path about 20 minutes—unless you linger, which is easy to do.

At rue Garneau ouest, if you're feeling energetic, turn left and climb up the hill to see, off to the left, a

15. fountain, sundial, and kiosk. The fountain was erected in 1967 to commemorate the 100th anniversary of Canadian confederation. The sundial, erected in 1987, honors the Astronomy Observatory in Québec City. Shows are performed in the kiosk in summer.

Return to the path, and soon you'll pass under:

16. Martello Tower no. 1, which you saw from a distance earlier in this walk. Note the round stones used in its construction.

As you continue along the pathway, look for burdock, aster, chicory, thistle, St. John's wort, goldenrod, and poison ivy; stay clear of the latter! Eventually you will arrive at the:

17. Grand Champlain Stairs, a steep stairway that leads to the base of the cliff. It's possible to climb down it to link up with rue Champlain and follow the sidewalk from here to the Lower Town and lively rue petit Champlain. However, for the purposes of this walk we'll stay in the park.

Beyond the stair, you'll head up the hill in a direction perpendicular to rue Ontario. You'll quickly arrive at another road and the Cap Diamant earthworks, built after General Montgomery's attack on Québec in 1775. Continue up the hill to another road and follow it (or the well-worn footpath; you won't be the first person to have passed this way) to a:

18. scenic lookout. Stretched out before you is the mighty St. Lawrence River and its pretty south shore (a popular area for excursions). There are rest rooms here, and this is a favorite stop along tour-bus routes.

To your left as you face the river, there is access to the:

19. Promenade des Gouverneurs, built from 1959 to 1960. The promenade hugs the side of the cliff and follows the silent stone walls of the Citadelle, bringing you back to the Old Town in about 20 minutes. The steps, some 310 in all, are wide and low for easy maneuvering, and rest areas are conveniently spaced along the way. (The promenade is dimly lit at night but safe; I walked it at dusk and found other people doing the same.) At

FREDERICK G. TODD

Battlefields Park, also known as the Plains of Abraham, was designed by landscape architect Frederick G. Todd, an American who made Québec his home early in his career. Born in 1876 in Concord, New Hampshire, Todd studied at the agricultural college in Amherst, Massachusetts, and then apprenticed with the well-known American landscape architect Frederick Law Olmsted from 1896 to 1900. (Olmsted laid out Montréal's Mont-Royal Park, Central Park in New York City, and many others.)

When he left Olmsted's firm, at the age of 24, Todd moved to Montréal and set up the first resident practice of landscape architecture in Canada. Following in the footsteps of his mentor and teacher, he created parks all over Canada and also pursued city planning and public works projects.

In 1903, he prepared a comprehensive report on future expansion for Ottawa, making proposals for parks, avenues, and boulevards that were later implemented. From 1904 to 1907, he created Assiniboine Park in Winnipeg, Manitoba, and Wascana Park in Regina, Saskatchewan. In 1908, he designed the township of Point Grey, in British Columbia; and in 1912 and 1913, Battlefields Park in Québec City.

Todd continued to design urban parks as well as private gardens and institutional grounds until 1930. From 1930 to 1940, he was involved in major public works projects that included the restoration of the historic buildings on Ile Ste-Hélène in Montréal and the creation on the island of one of the first playing fields for girls, to "provide Montréal's underprivileged citizens with a much needed rest and recreation center." In 1939, he created the well-loved and well-used Beaver Lake in Mont-Royal Park in Montréal—a project that had been a dream of Olmsted's more than 60 years earlier. Todd's last commission, from 1945 to 1948, was the creation of the Garden of the Way of the Cross beside St. Joseph's Oratory in Montréal.

An articulate, passionate, yet modest man, Frederick Todd died in Montréal in 1948; to this day, few people in Canada or the United States know of him despite the far-reaching legacy he left behind.

the last set of stairs, just above a turreted kiosk, you'll see, to your left, a:

20. **toboggan ramp** (les Glissades de la Terrasse), which has played a part, in one form or another, in the lives of the outdoors-loving Québécois since 1884. The Château Frontenac built its first ramp in 1915. The present one is owned by Parks Canada and run by a private operator. In winter, happy riders zip along this 270-foot (82-meter) incline at speeds up to 60 miles (90 kilometers) per hour. For added fun when the temperature drops, there is a skating rink nearby, and a sugar shack for making candy by wrapping maple syrup on a stick. Other times of the year, the skating rink and sugar shack disappear, and the ramp looks deserted and forlorn.

Follow the stairs down to:

21. **Terrasse Dufferin** (Dufferin Terrace), built around 1879 and looking much as it did then. It's easy to imagine women in long dresses and parasols and men with top hats and canes advancing toward you in the distance, silhouetted against the Château Frontenac.

As you stroll along the promenade towards the château, and the end of this tour, note the cannons on the lower level of the Parc des Gouverneurs. Four cannons are British, and two are Russian, trophies from the Crimean War. The cannons that originally stood here were powerful enough to reach their targets across the river.

REFUELING STOP Follow Terrasse Dufferin to the Château Frontenac, where you can pop into the lower level **café** for a pick-me-up. The entrance is near the Champlain monument. There are boutiques and rest rooms on this level, too.

For a meal in a more intimate dining setting, make your way to the main floor of the château and **Café de la Terrasse,** where you won't feel underdressed in your casual walking attire. The café hosts a popular buffet dinner and dancing on Saturday nights.

Lower Town & Old Port

Start: The funicular near the Château Frontenac.
Finish: Rue St-Paul and the antiques district.
Time: 2 hours, not counting museum-going or shopping.
Best Time: Weekdays, when most antiques shops are open (some are also open on Saturday afternoon); otherwise, shops in the Lower Town are open daily.

Québec City's Lower Town is even more compact, if that is imaginable, than its Upper Town. Quaint streets and 17th- and 18th-century houses are sandwiched between the historic Old Port and a steep cliff with the Château Frontenac, a constant presence, peeking over the top.

Here, in 1608, Samuel de Champlain founded a small settlement called l'Habitation. It was a location susceptible to attack: First by the Iroquois, who called this land *Kebec* and wanted the Europeans off it; then by the English, who coveted it from the French; and finally by the Americans, miffed that the French did not choose to join them in their war with the English.

Perhaps nowhere is Québec's colorful history more palpable than in the streets of the Lower Town and at its port, once one of the most important in the world.

Since most visitors to Québec City stay in the Upper Town, you'll probably start this tour from that part of the city. There are two methods of descending to the Lower Town. The easiest way is to hop aboard the:

1. **funicular,** on Terrasse Dufferin near the Château Frontenac. As you glide down the steep slope in the cable car, you'll be treated to a bird's-eye view of mammoth grain elevators—those rows of upright cylinders down in the harbor—with a capacity of eight million bushels; the harbor and the river; and the Laurentian Mountains rising in the distance.

   If you prefer a more active means of descent than the funicular, and a free one, use the stairs to the left of the funicular (as you face it), which link up with:

2. **Breakneck Stairs** (Escalier Casse-Cou), the name of which is self-explanatory once you see them. A stairway has existed here to help people scale the cliff since the settlement began: If you look at an early map—one drawn in 1660, say—you'll find the stairs represented. But human beings weren't the only ones to use the stairs. In 1698, the town council forbade citizens to take their animals up or down the stairway, or face a fine.

   Both Breakneck Stairs and the funicular will deposit you at the:

3. **Maison Louis Jolliet** (Louis Jolliet House), which now serves as the lower terminus for the funicular. Built in 1683, it was the home, until his death at age 55 in 1700, of the great Québec-born explorer. With Father Jacques Marquette, Jolliet was the first person of European parentage to explore the upper reaches of the Mississippi River. He is also known for exploring the Great Lakes and the Hudson Bay, but one thing few people know about him is that he was an organist, and he played for the Québec cathedral. A monument to the multitalented Jolliet stands beside the house.

   The Maison Jolliet became the lower terminus for the funicular in 1879. It faces rue Sous-le-Fort, which in modern times is lined with souvenir shops (there's a cash machine here, too), and is situated on lively pedestrian:

4. **rue du Petit-Champlain,** with this singular claim to fame: It is the oldest street in North America. It is also perennially thronged with restaurant-goers, café-sitters, strolling couples,

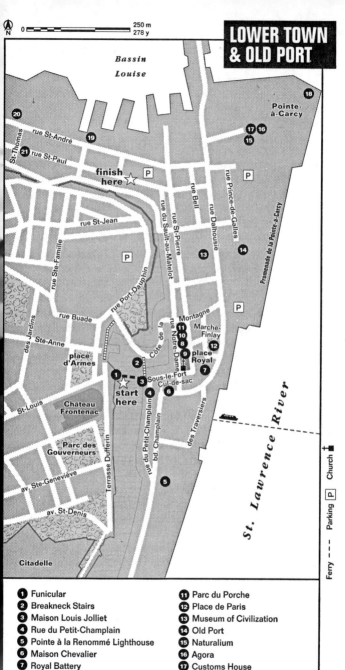

LOWER TOWN & OLD PORT

0 ————— 250 m
278 y

Bassin Louise

Pointe-à-Carcy

rue St-André

rue St-Paul

finish here ☆

rue St-Jean

rue Ste-Famille

rue Bell

rue du Sault-au-Matelot

rue St-Pierre

rue Dalhousie

rue Prince-de-Galles

Promenade de la Pointe-à-Carcy

rue Buade

rue Port-Dauphin

des Jardins

Ste-Anne

Montagne

Marché-Finlay

place d'Armes

Côte de la ap.

rue Notre-Dame

place Royal

St-Louis

start here ☆

Sous-le-Fort
Cul-de-sac

Château Frontenac

rue du Petit-Champlain

bd. Champlain

des Traversiers

Parc des Gouverneurs

Terrasse Dufferin

av. Ste-Geneviève

av. St-Denis

St. Lawrence River

Citadelle

Ferry - - - Parking ⓟ Church ✝∎

1 Funicular
2 Breakneck Stairs
3 Maison Louis Jolliet
4 Rue du Petit-Champlain
5 Pointe à la Renommé Lighthouse
6 Maison Chevalier
7 Royal Battery
8 Place Royale
9 Church of Notre-Dame-des-Victoires
10 Maison des Vins
11 Parc du Porche
12 Place de Paris
13 Museum of Civilization
14 Old Port
15 Naturalium
16 Agora
17 Customs House
18 Pointe-à-Carcy
19 Old Port Interpretation Center
20 Old Port Market
21 Rue St-Paul

and groups of school children out to absorb Québec history firsthand.

Make your way down the street, ricocheting from one appealing store to another as you go. At the end of this street, you'll turn left onto boulevard Champlain. Across the street stands an escapee from the Gaspé Peninsula, the:

5. **Pointe à la Renommé Lighthouse,** next to the Québec Coast Guard Base at the auto entrance to the Québec–Levis ferryboat. Erected on the Pointe à la Renommé on the Gaspé Peninsula in 1906, this lighthouse in the old St. Lawrence style took its name from a point of land, which, in turn, was named for a ship, the *Renommé,* that had run aground there in 1736.

A modern lighthouse was erected on Pointe à la Renommé in 1975, and this picturesque one was moved here. Its huge glass lenses represented the height of technology at the turn of the century.

Stroll along boulevard Champlain, past more shops and cafés, following the curve of the street, which will deposit you at the:

6. **Maison Chevalier** (Chevalier House), which was the home of merchant Jean-Baptiste Chevalier and dates from 1752. Note the wealth of windows in the house—more than 30 in the facade alone!

In 1763, the house was sold at auction to shipowner Jean-Louis Fremont, the grandfather of Virginia-born John Charles Fremont (1813–1890). John Charles was an American explorer, soldier, and politician who explored and mapped some 10 western and midwestern states. This busy man of French-Canadian heritage was also a governor of California and Arizona, a candidate for president of the United States in 1856, and a general during the Civil War.

The Chevalier House was sold in 1806 to an Englishman, who, in turn, rented it to a hotelier, who transformed it into an inn. From this time to the end of the century it was known, under various owners, as the London Coffee House. In 1960 the Québec government restored the house, and it became a museum about five years later, overseen by the Museum of Civilization, which mounts temporary exhibitions here.

REFUELING STOP Behind the Maison Chevalier is a wonderful little bakery with only a couple of tables and chairs. It's called **Boulangerie Dinan** (after owner Jim Dinan, one of an unusual breed, an Anglo Québécois), at 6 rue

Cul-de-Sac, and you can find it by walking up rue Notre-Dame and taking the first left; you'll see it on the right.

Here you can get pastries, French-style pizza, sandwiches, soup, croissants, and baguettes. The specialty is bread made with maple syrup, sold only by the loaf and a real "word-of-mouth" sensation. I heard about it from an enthusiastic tour guide, and I recommend it heartily.

From here, walk one block up rue Notre-Dame to rue Sous-le-Fort, turn right, and walk one more block to the:

7. Royal Battery, which was erected in 1691. The cannons were added in 1712 to defend the Lower Town. They got the chance in 1759, but the English victory at that time silenced them; the Lower Town was burned and its buildings destroyed by cannon balls and bombs.

The exodus to the Upper Town at this time left the city's own cannons to rust. Sunken foundations were all that remained of the Royal Battery by the turn of the century, and when the time came to restore this area, it had to be rebuilt from the bottom up.

From the Royal Battery, return to rue Sous-le-Fort and follow it one block to rue Notre-Dame. Turn right. Half a block up the grade is the heart of the Lower Town:

8. place Royale, site of the first permanent colony in New France. In the early days this was the bustling town marketplace, and today it has been restored to very near its old-time appearance. It had gone into decline around 1860 and by 1950 had become the derelict, rundown part of town.

At the core of the square is a bust of Louis XIV, the Sun King. A gift from the city of Paris in 1928, it was installed in 1931. Another bust of Louis XIV had stood here from 1686 to 1689, but it was removed at the urging of local merchants because it impeded the flow of traffic into and out of the busy market square.

The striking 17th- and 18th-century houses around the square once belonged to wealthy merchants; their stores were on the ground floor and they lived above them. Two of the houses on the square, Maison Fornel and Maison Bruneau-Rageot-Drapeau, become interpretation centers in summer, with exhibits and a multimedia display.

You'll find rest rooms in the shop at no. 21, which charges a small "admission fee."

Facing the square is the small:

9. Church of Notre-Dame-des-Victoires, the oldest stone

BENEDICT ARNOLD

Born in 1741 in Connecticut, Benedict Arnold became an American general who turned traitor during the American Revolutionary War. In fact, his name has become synonymous with that word.

In May 1775, while he was still committed to the American cause, Arnold and Ethan Allen captured the British-held Fort Ticonderoga. In November of the same year, at the behest of General George Washington, he marched an army of 700 strong through the Maine wilderness to attack Québec.

At that time, the Americans were angered by Québec's loyalty to the crown. Benjamin Franklin's urging the French-Canadians to join the Americans in their struggle had come to naught.

During the siege of Québec, Arnold was joined by the American General Richard Montgomery, and together they led an attack on the Lower Town on December 31, 1775. A snowstorm was raging that day, but if they had waited, they might have lost the reinforcement from American mercenaries, many of whose contracts would expire on January 1st.

In the end, it didn't make any difference. Montgomery was killed in the battle, but, despite being seriously wounded himself, Arnold continued to lay siege to the city until the spring, when British reinforcements arrived and rousted the Americans, Arnold included, once and for all.

Within four years, Benedict Arnold would become a turncoat. In 1778, he was placed in command of Philadelphia, where he socialized with people of Loyalist sympathies. He smarted at being passed over for promotion in the military, perhaps for the abuses of power he had shown. In 1779, he married a Loyalist sympathizer, Peggy Shippen.

In 1780, Arnold was given command of West Point, which he plotted to surrender to the British for £20,000. When his British partner in crime, Major John André, was captured by the Americans, Arnold fled to the British camp. André was hanged as a spy, and Benedict Arnold went into exile in 1781 in London, where he remained, ill and ostracized, until his death 20 years later.

church in Québec, built in 1688. The church became known as Notre-Dame-de-la-Victoire after the French defeat of Admiral William Phips in 1690; when Admiral Havenden Walker was defeated in 1711, the word "victory" became plural. In 1759 the church was destroyed by fire when the English defeated the French but was rebuilt within the same walls that you see now. It has been renovated twice, in 1888 and 1929, but has actually changed little over the years.

The paintings, castlelike altar, and large model boat suspended from the ceiling were votive offerings brought by early settlers to ensure safe voyages. The church is usually open to visitors during the day, unless a wedding is underway.

Across the square from the church stands the:

10. **Maison des Vins** (House of Wines), the primo wineshop of the Québec Société des Alcools. In the cool *voutes* (vaults) of the cellar of this old Québec City stone house are the best wines that the liquor monopoly has for sale. Whether or not you intend to buy, the Maison des Vins affords a good opportunity to explore the lower reaches of an old house, and to savor the cool darkness, a welcome diversion on a hot summer day.

Follow rue Notre-Dame a half a block farther and look to your right. You'll see a whimsical children's playground called:

11. **Parc du Porche.** The park, which is surrounded by picturesque stone houses, is put to good use by local small-fry with a penchant for climbing. A stylized ship, a rowboat, and cannons manage to occupy their interest, conjure up seafaring fantasies, and bow to history as well. There are wooden cutouts of French pioneers where kids can insert their own faces—just to complete the fantasy and provide a photo opportunity for their parents. If you've brought along a snack, you can eat it at a picnic table and benches supplied by the park.

Return to place Royale and walk down rue du Marché-Finlay to the:

12. **place de Paris,** with its maddeningly modern *Dialogue with History,* by French sculptor Jean-Pierre Raynaud, which commemorates the first French settlers in Québec. The piece was created in a language seemingly incompatible with that of the surrounding area, unlike the beautifully incorporated Museum of Civilization nearby.

Place de Paris was created in 1987, and in the summer an information center is open on the square in the renovated late-19th-century Thibaudeau warehouse, at 215 rue du Marché-Finlay.

> **REFUELING STOP** Walk a couple of short blocks to the popular local restaurant **Le Café du Monde,** at 57 rue Dalhousie two doors past rue de la Montagne. The moderately priced café is known for its imported beers, its selection of wines by the glass, and its large servings of mussels. It's fun, and the waiters dote on you.

From place de Paris (or Le Café du Monde), turn left onto rue Dalhousie and walk to the:

13. Museum of Civilization (Musée de la Civilisation), 86 rue Dalhousie just past St-Antoine. The museum, which opened in 1988, may be situated in the warren of cobblestoned streets in the historic Old City, but there is nothing old or remotely traditional about it. Modern, spacious, and airy, it is one of the most exciting and innovative museums in Canada, if not in all of North America. Exhibits make good use of computers and videos and appeal to adults and children alike. Most notable is the sprawling "Memoires" (Memories), a permanent exhibit that presents a time capsule of Québec history. Come back later if you can't visit the museum now, but do try to see it during your stay.

Across the street from the Museum of Civilization is the:

14. Old Port (Vieux-Port), a revitalized 72-acre riverfront area, which you may enter through the parking lot. In the 17th, 18th, and 19th centuries the port bustled with activity and ships going back and forth between Québec and Europe. The port went into decline in the early 20th century, but since the mid-1980s it has experienced a rebirth, becoming the summer destination for international cruise ships (you may see some on your walk), as well as the repository of museums, cafés, and a pretty pedestrian walkway.

When you get to the port promenade, turn left and stroll along it. Soon you'll come to one of the port's growing number of attractions, the:

15. Naturalium, a museum of natural sciences that opened in June 1993 to celebrate the bio-diversity on the planet, from beetles to bison. A private enterprise, Naturalium is the brainchild of "15 crazy businessmen in Québec City," as one of them puts it.

Guides stationed throughout can provide English explanations of the exhibits of insects, animals, and minerals from all over the world. (You may also ask for a printed English text when you pay your admission.)

Follow the paw prints from one exhibit to another. The taxidermy is excellent, from birds in flight to cheetah to arctic fox; out of the museum collection of 840 items, you can expect to see 160 displayed at any given time, though the rest are stored in plain view on the breezeway. On the upper levels there is an art gallery and a children's activity center.

Directly in front of the Naturalium is a small outdoor theater, and beside it the much larger:

16. Agora, with 6,000 seats and a clamshell-shaped stage. This is the city's largest open-air theater, and a popular choice for entertainment on balmy summer evenings.

From this vantage point, you can admire (but don't walk to—it's not open to the public) the striking building directly behind the Agora. It is the city's:

17. Customs House. The building, with half a dozen columns, was constructed in 1856 to replace the former customs house built between 1830 and 1839. The interior of the existing building was destroyed by fire in 1864. Fire struck again in 1909, destroying the original dome, which was replaced by the smaller one you see today.

To the right of the Customs House, the building with the copper clock tower is the administrative offices of the Port of Québec Corporation.

From the Agora, you can stroll out to the landscaped:

18. Pointe-à-Carcy. From here, you can look out across Louise Basin to see the Bunge of Canada grain elevator, which stores the grain (wheat, barley, corn, and soy beans) produced in western Canada before it is shipped to Europe. You might also see someone fishing off the pier. From here you can also see the bridge to rural Ile d'Orleans, which supplies much of Québec with fruits and vegetables.

From here, follow the walkway from Pointe-à-Carcy along the Louise Basin. If it is closed, as it was at this writing because of construction, follow the brick walkway toward the Customs House. On your right you'll see the city's new Navy School.

Walk around the Customs House to rue St-André. The small building behind it is the city's No. 6 Pump Station. From here, walk four not-especially-scenic blocks to rue Rioux.

On your right, at rue St-André and rue Rioux (or your left, if you have followed the pedestrian walkway along the Louise Basin), is a modern three-story building with blue trim, the:

19. Old Port Interpretation Center, at 100 rue St-André. The center reveals the Port of Québec City as it was in the 19th century, during its heyday. You'll learn all about that, as well as something about how people in Québec lived then.

Be sure to see the view of the port and the city from the top level of the Interpretation Center; handy reference maps will clarify what you see before you, including the Daishowa Pulp and Paper Mill (1927), which sells newsprint and cardboard to international markets. Among its customers for newsprint is the *New York Times*.

The Interpretation Center charges a small admission in summer, but at other times it's free. Texts are in English and French, and you're invited to touch most of the exhibits.

From the Old Port Interpretation Center, go to rue St-André, turn right, and walk one block to the:

20. Old Port Market (Marché du Vieux-Port), with its jaunty green roofs and blue banners. (From here you can also see the train station, circa 1916, designed by New York architect Bruce Price, who designed the Château Frontenac in 1893; can you see the resemblance?)

The colorful farmers' market teems with booths of fresh fruits and vegetables, relishes, jams, handicrafts, flowers, and honey from local hives. Above each booth hangs a sign with the name and telephone number of the seller; you'll see a lot bearing the initials "I.O.," meaning they come from picturesque Ile d'Orleans, 10 miles outside the city. The market is enclosed, and the central part of it, where you may buy meats and cheeses, is heated.

REFUELING STOP   There's a little café in the market where you can sit and enjoy a cup of coffee or a meal. The market also has an ice-cream stand and a bakery for a quick snack.

When you leave the market, cross rue St-André at the light and walk one short block to:

21. rue St-Paul, home to numerous antiques shops and cafés and reminiscent of streets in New York City's Greenwich Village. Turn left onto it and explore to your heart's content. Most of the shops stretch from rue Rioux, opposite the Interpretation Center, to rue du Sault-au-Matelot. There's a real sense of neighborhood here.

BOOM TIME

In the 17th century, the port of Québec served as the St. Lawrence beachhead for European ships bringing supplies and settlers to New France. About 60% of the exports from the new colony to France at that time were furs.

In 1786 the British parliament passed a law that all merchandise entering or leaving England be carried by ships built in British territory. This was good news for Québec, especially since England's war with the newly independent United States had resulted in the loss of many existing British ships.

From the beginning of the 19th century to about 1870, under British rule, the timber trade and shipbuilding took over in importance, and Québec reigned as one of the five most important ports in the world, along with Hong Kong, Sydney, London, and New York City. As many as 1,000 ships dropped anchor in Québec each year, and about twice that many ships were built at Québec, including the two largest ships afloat.

In 1806 Napoleon temporarily closed the Baltic ports to the English in a blockade, so England turned to its North American colonies to supply its timber. At the height of this era, between 1850 and 1869, almost 100 shipbuilders employed 5,000 workers. Lumberjacks floated oak and pine trees from the Ottawa Valley, known as "Great Britain's Warehouse," down the St. Lawrence River to Québec City on rafts the length of two or three football fields. With good reason, these rafts were known as "timber trains." Once the wood arrived, it would take two or three weeks to load it onto a ship.

All good things come to an end; by the early 20th century shipping had declined, and the economic power had shifted south to the port of Montréal.

For 19th-century European silver, porcelain, bronze, and lamps, duck into Antiquities Zaor at 112 rue St-Paul; for Québec and European furniture, Gerard Bourguet Antiquaire, 97 rue St-Paul; for silver, Renaud & Cie, 82 rue St-Paul; for folk art, Les Antiquites Marcel Bolduc, 79 rue St-Paul.

REFUELING STOP The popular neighborhood bistro **Restaurant-Café de Saint-Malo,** at 75 rue St-Paul and rue du Sault-au-Matelot, has low ceilings, rough stone walls, and storefront windows that just naturally draw you in. Come for a meal or, on sunny days, a drink or coffee and dessert at a sidewalk table.

From here you can wend your way back toward rue du Petit-Champlain for more browsing and soaking up the memorable ambience and architecture. Wander along rue du Sault-au-Matelot or rue St-Pierre. Pass by the corner of rues St-Pierre and St-Jacques; it was at this spot, in 1776, that Benedict Arnold was finally defeated by British reinforcements, ending the American general's long siege of the city.

I highly recommend a stop at the Librairie du Nouveau Monde (New World Bookstore), located at no. 103 St-Pierre. If this tour has piqued your interest in Québec's fascinating history, pick up a copy of the illustrated and highly readable *An Historical Guide to Québec,* by Yves Tessier, at the bookstore.

ESSENTIALS

This section corrals the practical information you'll need to make your stay in Montréal and Québec City fun and hassle-free. These "tips at your fingertips" include main thoroughfares, a primer on transit within the cities, and short A-to-Z–style guides to help you find what you need at a glance.

GETTING TO KNOW MONTREAL

MONTREAL ORIENTATION

CITY LAYOUT

At the risk of confusing you, let me say that Montréal is oddly laid out. Mark Twain had a point when he said that this is the only city where the sun sets in the north. Scrutinize a map of the city and you'll see that the streets labeled east (*est*) or west (*ouest*), such as rue Ste-Catherine or boulevard René-Lévesque, in reality run north (*nord*) and south (*sud*)—to be perfectly correct, northeast and southwest. To simplify things, I'll follow tradition, too, and refer to directions as the Montréalers do.

Main Streets & Arteries

In downtown Montréal, the principal streets running east–west include boulevard René-Lévesque, rue Ste-Catherine, boulevard de Maisonneuve, and rue Sherbrooke. The north–south arteries include rue Crescent; rue McGill; rue St-Denis; and boulevard St-Laurent, the line of demarcation between east and west Montréal (most of the downtown area you probably will visit lies in the west).

Near Mont-Royal Park, north of the downtown area, major streets are avenue du Mont-Royal and avenue Laurier.

In Old Montréal, rue St-Jacques (home to many banks), rue Notre-Dame, and rue St-Paul are the major streets, along with rue de la Commune, which hugs the St. Lawrence River.

GETTING AROUND MONTREAL

BY PUBLIC TRANSPORTATION

BY METRO For speed and economy, nothing beats Montréal's metro system. Long, modern, speedy trains whisk you through an ever-expanding network of underground tunnels for less than $2 a ride. A strip of six tickets represents more of a bargain. There are no discount passes or reduced fares for children.

Buy your tickets at the ticket window of any station, then slip one into the slot in the turnstyle to enter the system. Take a transfer (*correspondance*) from the machine just inside the turnstiles of every station, and this allows you to catch a bus at any other metro station for no extra fare. But remember to take your transfer at the station where you enter the system. (If you're starting your trip by bus and plan to continue on the metro, ask the bus driver for a transfer when you board.) If you need to change from one metro line to another, you'll most likely do it at the Berri-UQAM, Jean-Talon, or Snowdon stations (no transfer ticket necessary).

The metro runs from about 5:30am to midnight Sunday to Friday and until about 1am on Saturday.

BY BUS Buses cost the same as the metro, and metro tickets can be used on buses, too. If you pay the bus fare in cash rather than using metro tickets you'll need exact change. Though riding the buses is pleasant, and they run throughout the city, they aren't as frequent or as efficient as the metro. Whenever I've waited for a bus in Montréal, I've really *waited* for a bus.

BY TAXI

If you don't want to take public transportation, you'll be glad to find that there are plenty of taxis representing a variety of private companies. Most short rides from one point to another downtown cost $5 or $6. Tip about 15%. Your hotel staff can call a cab for you, or you can walk to any large hotel entry or transport terminal and get one on your own.

BY WATER TAXI

This is a fun way to get around part of Montréal, say from the Old Port to Ile Ste-Hélène and all its attractions or Ile Notre-Dame and the Montréal Casino. Pick up the Aqua-Taxi at Quai Jacques-Cartier at the Old Port.

BY CAR

If you drive to Montréal, or rent a car when you arrive, you may choose to drive to the push-off point for the walks you've chosen to

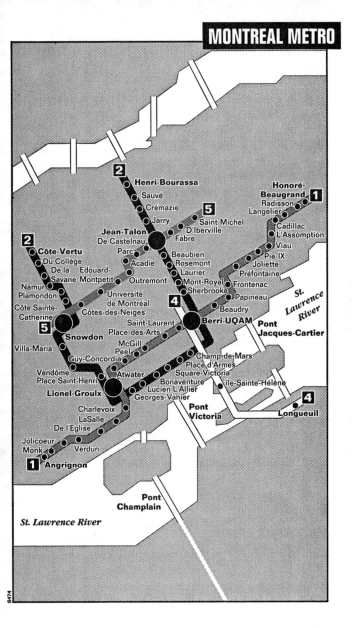

2 Henri-Bourassa
Sauvé
Crémazie
Jarry

2 Côte-Vertu
Du Collège
De la
Savane
Edouard-
Montpetit
Namur
Plamondon
Côte Sainte-
Catherine
5
Snowdon
Villa-Maria

Jean-Talon
De Castelnau
Parc
Acadie
Outremont
Université
de Montréal
Côtes-des-Neiges
Saint-Laurent
Place-des-Arts
McGill
Peel
Guy-Concordia
Vendôme
Place Saint-Henri
Lionel-Groulx
Atwater

5 Saint-Michel
D'Iberville
Fabre
Beaubien
Rosemont
Laurier
Mont-Royal
Sherbrooke
Beaudry
Berri-UQAM

Honoré-
Beaugrand **1**
Radisson
Langelier
Cadillac
L'Assomption
Viau
Pie-IX
Joliette
Préfontaine
Frontenac
Papineau

St.
Lawrence
River

Pont
Jacques-Cartier

Champ-de-Mars
Place d'Armes
Square-Victoria
Bonaventure
Lucien L'Allier
Georges-Vanier

île-Sainte-Hélène

4
Longueuil

Charlevoix
LaSalle
De l'Eglise
Jolicoeur
Monk
Verdun
1 **Angrignon**

Pont
Victoria

Pont
Champlain

St. Lawrence River

do. (Keep in mind that most of these walks aren't circular and don't deposit you back near where you started, so you'll usually have to return to your car by metro, bus, or taxi.)

Parking can be tough in downtown Montréal, which gets its share of traffic, but there are plenty of parking meters, and most downtown shopping complexes have underground parking lots, as do the big downtown hotels. Some hotels don't charge you extra to take your car in and out of the lot during the day, which can save you money if you plan to use your car a lot.

The Canadian Automobile Association, or CAA (tel. 514/861-7111 for information, or 514/861-1313 for emergencies), is affiliated with the American Automobile Association (AAA).

RENTALS   All the large, well-known car-rental agencies operate here or have affiliates (National, for instance, is represented in Canada by Tilden). Basic rates are about the same from company to company, and terms, cars, and prices resemble those in the United States. What can be a shock to visitors from the United States is the high cost of gasoline in Québec.

 MONTRÉAL

American Express   Offices of the American Express Travel Service are at 1141 rue de Maisonneuve ouest (tel. 384-3640) and at The Bay (La Baie) department store, 585 rue Ste-Catherine ouest, fifth floor (tel. 281-4777). For lost or stolen cards, call toll free 800/268-9824.

Area Code   The area code for Montréal is 514.

Banks   Hours vary from bank to bank, but most are open weekdays from 8:30am or 9am to 4pm or 5pm. Some are also open on Saturday. Inquire at your hotel or a tourist information office.

Bookstores   Montréal is rich in bookstores, many of which stock English-language books. The biggest is Coles, with many English titles, located downtown at 1171 rue Ste-Catherine ouest (tel. 849-8825). Champigny, 4380 rue St-Denis (tel. 844-2587), is a large, primarily French-language bookstore, with a vast selection—great for French teachers and students. For travel-related books, guidebooks, maps, and travel accessories, visit Ulysses, in the Latin Quarter at 4176 rue St-Denis near rue Duluth (tel. 289-9875); near the Delta Montréal Hotel at 560 avenue Président-Kennedy (tel. 843-7222); and on the lower level of Ogilvy department store, on rue Ste-Catherine at de la Montagne (tel. 842-7711, ext. 362). L'Androgyne, the gay, lesbian, and feminist bookstore at 3636 boulevard St-Laurent (tel. 842-4765), has books in both French and English.

Business Hours Store hours are 9am to 6pm Monday through Wednesday; 9am to 9pm on Thursday and Friday; and 9am to 5pm on Saturday. Many stores now open on Sunday from noon to 5pm.

Climate The best months for walking around Montréal are May to October. Spring is short but sweet and carpets the city with tulips and lilacs. Summer, from mid-June through mid-September, is a dependably fun time, but the time of real magnificence has got to be autumn (mid-September and October), with days that are still warm and the world-famous Canadian maples ablaze with color. Montreal winters can be cold and harsh, but a wealth of winter sports—and the city's winter carnival—keep the city lively through-out the season.

Currency Exchange There are currency exchange offices just where you're likely to need them most: at the airport, in the train station, on place Jacques-Cartier in Old Montréal, and in Infotouriste at Dorchester Square.

Emergencies Dial 911 for the police, firefighters, or an ambulance; for a dental emergency, call 342-4444.

Etiquette The magic words—*excusez-moi, s'il vous plaît,* and *merci*—work wonders here. The Québécois are a polite, gracious lot; you'll hear *excusez* (short for *excusez-moi*) on the street all the time.

Libraries The Québec National Library (La Bibliothèque Nationale du Québec), a research facility in a striking building with stained-glass windows, is at 1700 rue St-Denis in the Latin Quarter; it is a quiet place to read or riffle through the genealogy section where you can trace relatives you have (or have had) in this part of the world. It's open weekdays in summer, and Tuesday through Saturday the rest of the year; call for hours (tel. 873-1100).

Lost Property If you lose something in the metro, call 280-4637. If you leave something in a taxi, call the company you used and tell them when and where the driver picked you up.

Newspapers and Magazines Montréal's prime English-language newspaper is the *Montréal Gazette.* Most large newsstands and those in the larger hotels also carry the *Wall Street Journal,* the *New York Times, USA Today,* and the *International Herald Tribune,* as does the bookstore Champigny (see "Bookstores," above). For information about current happenings in Montréal, pick up the *Gazette,* or the free monthly booklet called *Montréal Scope,* available in some shops and hotel lobbies.

Rest Rooms With so many shopping complexes throughout

the city, you'll never be far from a bathroom. If you are stuck, go into a café and buy a cup of coffee so you won't feel guilty about using the facilities. If you don't feel guilty, ask if there is a pay telephone; the toilet is usually nearby.

Taxes Most goods and services in Canada are taxed 7% by the federal government. On top of that, the province of Québec adds an additional 8% tax on goods and services, and, since summer 1992, a 4% tax on hotels. In Québec, the federal tax is called—and appears on the bill as—the TPS (in other parts of Canada, it's called the GST); the provincial tax is known as the TVQ.

Tourists may receive a rebate on both the federal and provincial tax on items they have purchased but not used in Québec, as well as on lodging. To take advantage of this, you have to fill out necessary forms (ask for them at duty-free shops and hotels) and submit them, with the original receipts, within a year of the purchase. Contact the Canadian consulate or Québec tourism office for up-to-the-minute information about taxes and rebates. And save those receipts.

Telephones The telephone system, operated by Bell Canada, resembles the American system. All operators (dial "0" to talk with one) speak French and English, and will respond in your language as soon as they hear it. Pay phones in Québec require 25¢ for a 3-minute local call. Directory information calls (dial 411) are free. From hotels, calls usually cost more, be they local or long distance. Directories *(annuaires des téléphones)* come in white pages for residential numbers and yellow pages for commercial numbers.

Tipping Practices are similar to those in the United States: 15% on restaurant bills, 15% for taxi drivers, $1 per bag for porters and bellhops, $1 per night for the hotel room attendant. Hairdressers and barbers expect 10% to 15%. Hotel doormen should be tipped at your discretion for calling a taxi or helping in other ways.

Tourist Information A lot of beautifully prepared information about Montréal, Québec City, and environs is available, and the province of Québec and the individual cities are happy to share it with you.

The main information center for visitors to Montréal is the large and impressively organized Infotouriste, at 1001 rue du Square-Dorchester, between rues Peel and Metcalfe in the downtown hotel and business district (take the metro to Peel to get there). The local number is 873-2015; you can reach them toll-free from anywhere in Canada and the United States by calling 800/363-7777.

Employed by the Québec Ministry of Tourism, staff workers are extremely knowledgeable—and bilingual—and the center is an invaluable information resource regarding dining, accommodations, and attractions in Montréal and throughout the province. It can provide currency exchange, hotel bookings, and car rentals.

In Old Montréal, adjacent to place Jacques-Cartier, there is a city information center at 174 rue Notre-Dame est, at the corner of rue Notre-Dame and place Jacques-Cartier, near the monument to Lord Nelson.

Transit Information   Dial "AUTOBUS" (tel. 288-6287) for information about the metro and city buses. For airport transportation to Dorval or Mirabel, call Autocar Connaisseur/Gray Line (tel. 934-1222). For the Aqua-Taxi, making stops at the Old Port, Ile Notre-Dame, Ile Ste-Hélène, and the Longueil Yacht Club, call 891-6533.

GETTING TO KNOW QUEBEC CITY

Expect to spend all or almost all your time in Québec's Old City because most of the hotels, restaurants, attractions, entertainment, and tourist-oriented services are based there.

QUEBEC CITY ORIENTATION
CITY LAYOUT

Colonial Québec City, called the Lower Town today, was founded beside the St. Lawrence River at the foot of Cap Diamant (Cape Diamond). Here merchants, traders, and boatmen earned their livelihoods. But due to unfriendly fire in the 1700s, residents moved to a safer location atop Cap Diamant, now known as the Upper Town, and surrounded themselves with a stone wall.

This division into Upper and Lower Towns has persisted for obvious topographical reasons. The Upper Town remains enclosed by the Old City's fortification walls, and several ramplike streets and a cliffside elevator, called the funicular, connect it to the Lower Town.

Main Streets & Arteries

In the Old City, the main streets of the Upper City are St-Louis, which is the address of the Château Frontenac (it becomes the Grande Allée outside the city walls and leads to the Plains of Abraham), Ste-Anne, and St-Jean. Terrasse Dufferin overlooks the river and is for pedestrians only. In the Lower City, major streets include Petit-Champlain and Champlain, St-Pierre, Dalhousie, St-Paul and, parallel to it, St-André.

GETTING AROUND QUEBEC CITY

Getting around is simple in Québec City: Just walk, and with the help of this guide you'll be able to cover just about everything there is to see. Virtually no place of interest—or hotel or restaurant—is far away. If it's raining hard, or if it's slushy and you've left your waterproof boots at home, you may be obliged to take a bus or the occasional taxi, but in general your own two feet provide the best way to explore the city.

BY PUBLIC TRANSPORTATION

Although you can walk between the Château Frontenac (at the top of the cliff) and place Royale (at the bottom of the cliff), you can also allow yourself the luxury of a ride on, and a memorable view from, the **funicular,** which has been gliding up and down the cliff face along a 210-foot track for more than 100 years. The short trip costs about $1, and the car operates daily from 8am to midnight in summer (to 11:30pm in winter). The upper station is just off Terrasse Dufferin near the front of the Château Frontenac and place d'Armes; the lower station, in Maison Louis-Jolliet, is on popular rue du Petit-Champlain, and only a block or two from place Royale.

Local **buses** run quite often (something Québec City has over Montréal) and take exact change only. The no. 7 bus travels up and down rue St-Jean; no. 11, Grande Allée/rue St-Louis (this bus, along with nos. 7 and 8, also goes to Ste-Foy, in case you want to hit the big shopping centers there).

BY TAXI

Taxis are everywhere—cruising or parked in front of the big hotels outside the city gates—and they can be expensive. A local cab ride (from the Québec Museum or the railway station to the Château Frontenac, say) will run you about $6.

BY CAR

You don't really need a car if you plan to stay only in Québec City, but if you choose to rent one, you'll find major car-rental companies at the airport and in the Old City. On-street parking is a problem in the cramped quarters of the Old City. Should you be so lucky as to find a space on the street, check the signs for hours that parking is permissible; where meters are concerned, you pay 25¢ per 15 minutes up to 120 minutes. You may park free in a metered spot on Sunday *but not on Saturday.*

Many of the smaller hotels have special arrangements with local lots, which results in a discount for their guests, so check in at your hotel before you stick your car in a lot. There are plenty of parking lots clearly marked on the fold-out city map available at tourist offices. Several convenient ones include the Hôtel de Ville (City Hall), where parking is free in the evening and on weekends; Complexe G, off the Grande Allée on rue St-Cyrille, where you can take your car in and out of the lot two times a day at no extra charge; and in the Lower Town across the street from the Museum of Civilization, on rue Dalhousie, where discounts are often offered on weekends.

The Canadian Automobile Association, or CAA (tel. 418/624-2424 for information, 418/624-4000 for emergencies), is affiliated with the American Automobile Association (AAA).

FAST QUEBEC CITY

American Express There is no office right in town; see "Fast Facts: Montréal," above, for information on the office there.

Area Code The area code for Québec City is 418.

Bookstores Most of Québec City's bookstores cater to the solidly French-speaking citizenry and the horde of students at the university. A few shops, however, do carry English-language books for the tourist trade, such as Librairie Garneau, 24 Côte de la Fabrique (tel. 692-4262). Librairie du Nouveau Monde, 103 rue St-Pierre in Old Québec (tel. 694-9475), features a wide range of titles dealing with Québec history and culture, including books in English. Librairie Pantoute, 1100 rue St-Jean, sometimes carries copies of *French for Travellers*. For travel books, visit Ulysses, 4 boulevard René-Lévesque est (tel. 529-5349).

Banks Banks are open weekdays from 10am to 3pm, and most also have hours on Thursday and Friday evenings. Several banks have Saturday hours, but the ones that do are generally located outside of the Old Town.

Business Hours Store hours are 9:30am to 5:30pm Monday through Wednesday, 9:30am to 9pm on Thursday and Friday, 9:30am to 5pm on Saturday, and noon to 5pm on Sunday. Hours are often longer—from 9am to 9pm most days—in summer to take advantage of tourist traffic.

Climate   The climate of Québec City tends to be similar (perhaps 2 or 3 degrees cooler) to that of Montréal (see above). As in Montréal, the best months for walking around Québec City are May to October. (By October, you'll need a sweater or coat and sometimes a hat and gloves.)

Currency Exchange   Conveniently located near the Château Frontenac, the *bureau de change* at 19 rue Ste-Anne and rue des Jardins is open Monday, Tuesday, and Friday from 10am to 3pm, and Wednesday and Thursday from 10am to 6pm.

Emergencies   Police and fire, tel. 691-6911; Marine Search and Rescue (Canadian Coast Guard), tel. 648-3599 (Greater Québec Area) or toll free 800/463-4393 (St. Lawrence River).

Etiquette   See "Fast Facts: Montréal," above.

Newspapers and Magazines   Québec City's English-language newspaper, the *Chronicle-Telegraph,* is the equivalent of a small-town weekly newspaper. Founded in 1764, it claims to be North America's oldest newspaper. It's published on Wednesday, and the content is basically local news and advertisements. Broader-scope Canadian and American English-language newspapers and magazines are available at newsstands in the large hotels.

Rest Rooms   You'll find rest rooms in the tourist offices and on the ground floor of the commercial complex at 41 rue Couillard, in the Upper Town just off rue St-Jean (it's wheelchair accessible). In the Lower Town, one of the souvenir shops at place Royale makes its rest room available for 25¢; look for the sign out front. If you want to use the toilets at a café you pass, remember that many situate their rest rooms near the pay telephone.

Taxes   See "Fast Facts: Montréal," above.

Telephones   See "Fast Facts: Montréal," above.

Tipping   By all means, do. Waiters, waitresses, and cabbies appreciate a 10% to 15% tip; give bellhops $1 to carry a bag or two. The hotel doorman who hails your cab also deserves some coins in gratitude.

Tourist Information   The Greater Québec Area Tourism and Convention Bureau operates two well-staffed provincial tourist information centers, open year-round. One is in the old part of Québec City at 60 rue d'Auteuil, (tel. 418/692-2471). The other is in suburban Ste-Foy, at 3005 boulevard Laurier, which is near the Québec and Pierre-Laporte bridges (tel. 418/651-2882). Hours for both centers are daily from 8:30am to 8pm June to early September; daily from 8:30am to 5:30pm early September to mid-October;

weekdays Friday 9am to 5pm mid-October to mid-April; and 8:30am to 5:30pm mid-April to June.

The Québec Government's Tourism Department operates a city information office on place d'Armes, down the hill from the Château Frontenac, at 12 rue Ste-Anne (tel. 418/873-2015, a local call from Montréal, or toll free 800/363-7777 from other parts of Québec, Canada, and the United States). It's open June 10 to early September daily from 8:30am to 7:30pm, the rest of the year daily from 9am to 5pm; closed Christmas, New Year's Day, and Easter. The office has brochures for the entire province, as well as handy toilets. Across the hall in the same building are travel and car-rental agencies, cruise and bus-tour operators, a 24-hour instant teller, a currency-exchange office, and a free accommodations reservation service. In summer only, a small tourist office is open in the Lower Town at place Royale.

Parks Canada operates an information kiosk in front of the Château Frontenac; it's open daily from 9am to noon and from 1pm to 5pm. Walking tours to the Citadelle leave from here.

Transit Information Call 627-2511 for transit information.

RECOMMENDED READING

Some of the books recommended here may be difficult to find in bookstores in the United States, but you may order them through the mail-order house Exportlivre, C.P. 307, Saint-Lambert, Québec J4P 3P8 (tel. 514/671-3888; fax 514/671-2121). Contact the company to see if the books you're interested in are in stock.

HISTORY

Collard, Edgar Andrew, *Montreal Yesterdays* (The Gazette, 1989); *100 More Tales from All Our Yesterdays* (The Gazette, 1990).
Fournier, Me Rodolphe, *Lieux et monuments historiques de Québec et environs* (Editions Garneau Québec, 1976); available in French only.

Heritage Branch–Montreal, of the United Empire Loyalist Association of Canada, *The Loyalists of Québec—1774–1825* (Price-
Patterson Ltd., 1989).

Prevost, Robert; translated by Elizabeth Mueller and Robert Chodos,
Montreal—A History (McClelland and Stewart, 1993).

Rybczynski, Witold, et al., *McGill: A Celebration* (McGill-Queen's
University Press, 1991).

Tessier, Yves, *Historical Guide to Québec City* (Federation des
sociétés d'histoire du Québec, 1985).

Wolfe, Joshua, and Cecile Grenier, *Discover Montréal* (Libre Ex-
pression, 1991).

SOCIOLOGY

Lazar, Barry, and Douglas Tamsin, *Guide to Ethnic Montréal*
(Vehicule Press, revised edition, 1993).

Richler, Mordecai, *Home Sweet Home: My Canadian Album*
(Knopf, 1984; paperback, Penguin 1985).

Young, Brian, and John A. Dickinson, *A Short History of Québec: A
Socio-Economic Perspective* (Copp Clark Pitman Ltd., 1988).

GUIDEBOOKS

Choko, Marc H.; translated by Kathe Roth, *The Major Squares of
Montréal* (Meridian Press, 1990).

Remillard, Francois, et al., *Guide de Voyage Ulysse: Montréal*
(Editions Ulysse, 1993).

FICTION

Cohen, Leonard, *Beautiful Losers* (Viking, 1966).

Ethier-Blais, *White Desert* (Vehicule Press, Montréal, 1991).

Richler, Mordecai, *The Apprenticeship of Duddy Kravitz* (Knopf,
1959); *St. Urbain's Horseman* (Knopf, 1971); *Joshua Then &
Now* (Knopf, 1980).

Roy, Gabrielle, *The Tin Flute* (McClelland and Stewart, Toronto,
1980); published in French as *Bonheur d'occasion,* 1945. Other
books by Roy in English translation include *Street of Riches,
Children of My Heart, Where Nests the Water Hen, Windflow-
er, Enchanted Summer,* and *Garden in the Wind.*

Tremblay, Michel, *The Fat Woman Next Door Is Pregnant* (in
French by Lemeac, Montréal, 1978; in English by Talon Books,
1981); *Thérèse and Pierette and the Little Hanging Angel* (in
French by Lemeac, 1980; in English by Talon Books, 1984); both
from the four-volume *Plateau Mont-Royal Chronicles.*

ARCHITECTURE

Remillard, Francois, and Brian Merrett, *Montréal Architecture, A Guide to Styles and Buildings* (Meridian, Montréal, 1990).

Richards, Larry, editor, *Canadian Centre for Architecture: Building and Gardens* (Canadian Centre for Architecture, 1989, 1992; distributed by The MIT Press).

Index

Agora (open-air theater), 143
Aldred Building, 18
Algonquins, 5
Allen, Ethan, 6, 140
American Express office, 152
American Revolutionary War, 18
André, John, 140
Antiques Puces-Libre, 98
Antiques, shopping for
  in Montréal, 34, 98
  in Québec City, 144–45
Arnold, Benedict, 6, 118–19, 140, 146
Artefact (gallery), 98
Atwater Market, 32–33
Avenue Cartier, 129
Avenue Laval, 100
Avenue McGill College, 68–69

Baillairgé, Charles, 118, 128
Baillairgé Pavilion, 128
Bank of Montréal, 18–19
Banque du Commerce, 67
Barbeau Montréal, 96
Basilica Notre-Dame-de-Québec, 114–15
Battlefields Park (Parc des Champs-de-Bataille), 3–4, 45, 121, 126, 129–31

Battle of Québec (1759), 3–4, 117, 129–30
Bay, The (La Baie), 74, 76
Beaver Lake (Lac des Castors), 49
Biodome, 36, 38
Birks, Henry, 77
Boat ramp (Old Montréal to Ile Ste-Hélène), 88–89
Bonhomme Carnaval (mascot), 125
Bonsecours Basin Park, 28
Books about Montréal and Québec City, 159–61
Bookstores
  in Montréal, 77, 81, 98, 152
  in Québec City, 157
Botanical Garden, 39–41
Boulevard René-Lévesque, 54
Boulevard St-Laurent, 102, 104
Bourgeoys, Marguerite, 12, 15
Bourget, Ignace, 56
Breakneck Stairs (Escalier Casse-Cou), 136
Brossad, Georges, 40

Calder, Alexander, 86
Calvet, Pierre du, 12

Canadian Centre for Architecture (CCA), 70–72
Canadiens (ice-hockey team), 8
Cannonball (from War of 1759), 117
Cap Diamant (Cape Diamond), 2–3, 109
Cars and driving
  in Montréal, 150–52
  in Québec City, 156–57
Cartier, Jacques, 2, 4, 30
Cartier, Sir George-Etienne, 105, 106
Cathédrale Marie-Reine-du-Monde (Cathedral of Mary, Queen of the World), 56
Centaur Theater, 19
Centre de Commerce Mondial, 62, 64
Centre d'Histoire de Montréal, 22
Chalet Lookout, 49–50
Champigny (bookstore), 98
Champlain, Hélène de, 92
Champlain, Samuel de, 2, 92, 110, 113, 135
Chapel of the Sacred Heart, 17
Château de Ramezay, 16
Château Dufresne, 42–43
Château Frontenac, 113–14
Chateil, Serge, 91
Chevalier, Jean-Baptiste, 138
Chinese Garden, 40–41
Christ Church Cathedral, 56–57
Church of Notre-Dame-des-Victoires, 139, 141
Citadelle, 118–19
City Hall (Hôtel-de-Ville)
  in Montréal, 16–17
  in Québec City, 115
Cloister Garden (place de la Cathédrale), 69
Closse, Raphael-Lambert, 18
Coles (bookstore), 81, 152
Corriveau, Marie-Josephte, 130
Cours Mont-Royal, Les, 80–81
Customs House, 143

D'Astous, Roger, 67
Daudelin, Charles, 17
David M. Stewart Museum, 90
Decorative Arts Museum, 42–43
Desmarais, Paul, 62
Dickens, Charles, 14, 109
Dickinson, Peter, 67
Dinasaurium, 92
Dorchester Square, 54
Dorval, Charles, 128
Dufferin, Lord, 110
Dufresne, Oscar and Marius, 42
D'Youville, Marguerite, 15, 22

Eaton, Timothy, 78, 79
Eaton Centre, 78–79
Eglise Notre-Dame-de-Bonsecours, 12
Eisenhower, Dwight D., 56
Elizabeth II, Queen of England, 56, 83, 119

Farine Five Roses (flour mill), 31
Fast Facts
  for Montréal, 152–55
  for Québec City, 157–59
Faugeron, Jean, 91
Floral Park (Jardins des Floralies), 91
Fortin, Louis, 128
Fortin, Marc-Aurele, 22
Fortress of Ile Ste-Hélène, 90
François Decarie (milliner), 98
Franklin, Benjamin, 6, 12, 16, 140
Fremont, John Charles, 138
Frontenac, Louis de Buade, Comte de, 114
Fuller, Buckminster, 89
Funicular (Terrasse Dufferin), 136, 156

Gage, Thomas, 3–4
Gaspé, Philippe Aubert de, 112
Geodesic dome, 89
George III, King of England, 18, 116
Georges Laoun (optician), 99
Gladstone, Gerald, 56, 68
Grand Champlain Stairs, 131
Grande Allée, 121–29
Gray Nuns General Hospital, 22
Greenhouses (serres), 41
Griffintown, 31
Guimard, Hector, 64

Harbor Bridge, 88
Hébert, Henri, 41
Hébert, Louis-Philippe, 56, 115, 124
Henderson, William Samuel, 83
Henry Birks et Fils, 77
Hill, George William, 105
History of Montréal and Québec City, 2–8
Holt, John, 83
Holt Renfrew, 83–84
Holy Trinity Anglican Cathedral, 116
Hôpital Général, 15
Hôtel-de-Ville (City Hall)
  in Montréal, 16–17
  in Québec City, 115
Hôtel-Dieu-de-Montréal, 5, 15
Hotel Rasco, 14
Hudson's Bay Company, 74, 76

IBM-Marathon Building, 64, 66–67
Ile Notre-Dame, 86, 90–93
Ile Ste-Hélène (St. Helen's Island), 85–90
Illuminated Crowd, The (sculpture), 59, 70
Incarnation, Marie de l', 116, 117, 125
Information sources. *See* Tourist information
Insectarium, 39–40
International Fireworks Competition, 90
Inuits, 60
Iroquois, 2, 4, 5, 17–18, 135

Jacques-Cartier Bridge, 88
Japanese Pavillion and Garden, 40
Jardin Jeanne d'Arc (Joan of Arc Garden), 126
Jeanne Mance Park, 105
Jolliet, Louis, 136

Kennedy, John, 33
Kipling, Rudyard, 2, 109

Lachine Canal, 30–31
Laliberté, Alfred, 17
Lambert, Phyllis, 71
Language, 8
La Ronde (amusement park), 90
LaSalle, Jules, 17
Laurentian Bank Building, 70
Laval, François-Xavier, 115
Laval University, 115
Leclerc, Félix, 99
Lemoyne, Charles, 17
Levasseur, Pierre-Noel, 116
La Vieille Europe (Old Europe), 104
Liberte, Father Firmia, 40
L'Incarnation, Marie de, 116, 117, 125
Louis XIV, King of France, 114, 139
Lower Town, 2, 135–43

McCord, David Ross, 59
McCord Museum of Canadian History, 59–60
MacDonald, Sir John A., 54
McGill, James, 59, 68
McGill University, 59, 68
Madison, James, 7
Maison Bruneau-Rageot-Drapeau, 139
Maison Calvet (Calvet House), 12
Maison Chevalier (Chevalier House), 138
Maison des Vins (House of Wines)
    in Montréal, 77
    in Québec City, 141

Maison Fornel, 139
Maison Henry-Stuart, 129
Maison Jacquet (Jacquet House), 112
Maison Kent (Kent House), 112
Maison Louis Jolliet (Louis Jolliet House), 136
Maison Maillou (Maillou House), 112–13
Maisonneuve, Paul de Chomeday, Sieur de, 5, 17
Maison Smith (Smith House), 48–49
Mance, Jeanne, 5, 15, 17
Manoir d'Esplanade, 117
Man (sculpture), 86
Marché Bonsecours (Bonsecours Market), 12, 14
Marie Guyart Building, 125
Marie-Victorin, Brother, 39, 42
Martello Towers, 126–27
    no. 1, 131
    no. 2, 126–27
Martin, Abraham, 129
Martineau, Aline, 128
Mason, Raymond, 59, 70
Metro travel, 149–50, 151
Military Drill Hall, 125
Molson, John, 29
Montcalm, Louis Joseph, Marquis de, 2–4, 116, 130
Montgomery, Richard, 6, 18, 118–19, 140
Montréal Casino, 91–92
Montréal Expos, 8
Mont-Royal Park, 4, 5, 45–51
Monument to the Faith, 113
Moore, David, 128
Moretti, Luigi, 64
Morgan, Henry, 74
Morin, Jacques, 49
Mot, André de, 91
Musée des Beaux-Arts (Museum of Fine Arts), 57–59, 83
Musée Marc-Aurele Fortin, 22
Museum of Archaeology and History, 20
Museum of Civilization (Musée de la Civilisation), 142

Naturalium (Museum of Natural Science), 142–43
Nelson, Lord Horatio, 14
Nervi, Pier, 64
New York Life Insurance Building, 18
Nincheri, Guido, 42
Nordheimer Building, 64
Notre-Dame Basilica, 17

Notre-Dame-des-Neiges Cemetery, 46, 49

Obelisk (Pointe-à-Callière), 21
O'Donnell, James, 17
Ogilvy, James Angus, 81–82
Old Court House, 17
Old Customs House, 20
Old Exchange Building, 19
Old Montréal, 4–5, 11–23
Old Port (Vieux-Port)
    in Montréal, 25–34
    in Québec City, 142
Old Port Interpretation Center, 143–44, 145
Old Port Market (Marché du Vieux-Port), 144
Olier, Jean-Jacques, 19
Olmsted, Frederick Law, 45–46, 48, 132
Olympic Park, 35–39
Olympic Tower, 38–39
1000 de la Gauchetière, 64, 66
Orientation
    to Montréal, 149
    to Québec City, 155–56

Parc des Ecluses (Locks Park), 30
Parc des Gouverneurs (Governors' Park), 110
Parc du Porche, 141
Parc Hélène-de-Champlain, 89–90
Parc Lafontaine, 99–100
Parliament Building (Hôtel du Parlement), 124
Pei, I. M., 56, 68
Phips, William, 114, 141
Pigeonier (pigeon house), 125
Place Bonaventure, 65–66
Place d'Armes, 5, 17–18, 113
Place de la Cathédrale, 69–70
Place de Paris, 141
Place Jacques-Cartier, 14–16
Place Montreal Trust, 79–80
Place Royale, 5, 139
Place Vauquelin, 17
Place Victoria, 64
Place Ville-Marie, 7, 56, 67–68, 79
Plage de l'Ile Notre-Dame, 92–93
Plains of Abraham, 3–4, 5, 121, 126, 129–31
Plateau Mont-Royal, 95–100
Pointe-à-Callière, 20
Pointe-à-Carcy, 143
Pointe à la Renommé Lighthouse, 138
Poitras, Jean-Claude, 82
Port of Montréal, 33
Port of Québec, 145

Pothier, Jean-Paul, 67
Power Corporation Building, 62
Price, Bruce, 114
Promenade des Gouverneurs, 110, 131
Promenades de la Cathédrale, Les, 78
Promenades du Vieux Québec, Les, 114

Quai Alexandra, 30
Quai de Brumes, 96
Quai de l'Horloge, 28
Quai Jacques-Cartier, 28
Quai King-Edward, 28–29
Québec Ministry of Finance, 113
Québec Museum, 127–28
Québec Seminary, 115
Queen Elizabeth Hotel, 56

Radisson Hotel, 65
Ramezay, Claude de, 16, 112
Rasco, Francisco, 14
Raynaud, Jean-Pierre, 141
Recollets monks, 113
Recommended reading, 159–61
Redpath Museum, 59
Regimental Goat, 118
Renard, Jules, 42
Renfrew, G. R., 83
Requin Chagrin (vintage clothing shop), 98
Rose, Peter, 68, 71, 72
Rose Garden, 41
Rotary (monument), 127
Royal Bank of Canada, 56, 68
Royal Battery, 139
Royal 22nd Regiment, 118–19
Rue Crescent, 57
Rue Duluth, 104–5
Rue du Petit-Champlain, 136, 138
Rue du Tresor, 114
Rue Prince-Arthur, 102
Rue St-Paul, 144–45
Rue Ste-Catherine, 57

Safdie, Moshe, 21, 58
Saguenay Marine Park, 39
Sailors' Church, 12
St. Lawrence Seaway, 31
St-Louis Gate, 118
St-Louis Square, 100, 102
Saint Pierre, Marie, 76
Schwartz's Montréal Hebrew Delicatessen, 104
Shaughnessy House, 71
Steel cross (Mont-Royal), 50
Stock Exchange Tower, 64–65
Sulpician Seminary, 19

Sun Life Building, 54, 67

Tache, Eugene-Etienne, 113, 125
Tailibert, Roger, 36
Taschereau, Elzear Alexandre, 115
Taxis
  in Montréal, 150
  in Québec City, 156
Terrasse Dufferin (Dufferin Terrace),
  4, 110, 133
Thêatre de Verdure, 100
Tintin (cartoon character), 96
Toboggan ramp (les Glissades de la
  Terrasse), 133
Todd, Frederick G., 130, 132
Tour de l'Ile (bicycle race), 58
Tourist information
  in Montréal, 16, 54, 80, 86,
    154–55
  in Québec City, 117, 158–59
Transportation
  in Montréal, 149–52, 155
  in Québec City, 156–57
Tremblay, Michel, 96, 160
Trudeau, Yves, 88–89

Ulysses (bookstore), 77, 152

Underground City, 80
United States Consulate, 110, 112
Upper Town, 2, 4, 109–19
Ursuline Convent, 116, 118
Ursuline Museum and Chapel, 116

Vauquelin, Jean, 17
Vielle Europe, La (Old Europe), 104
Victoria, Queen of England, 64, 83,
  119

Wade, George, 54
Walker, Havenden, 141
Washington, George, 6, 140
Whales, endangered, 39
White, Stanford, 19
Windsor Hotel, 54
Winter Carnival, 124, 125
Wolfe, James, 2–4, 127, 130
World Trade Centre (Centre de
  Commerce Mondial), 62, 64

Youville Stables, 21

Zeckendorf, William, 68

AC1

Please Send Me the Books Checked Below:

FROMMER'S COMPREHENSIVE GUIDES
(Guides listing facilities from budget to deluxe,
with emphasis on the medium-priced)

	Retail Price	Code		Retail Price	Code
☐ Acapulco/Ixtapa/Taxco 1993–94	$15.00	C120	☐ Morocco 1992–93	$18.00	C021
☐ Alaska 1994–95	$17.00	C131	☐ Nepal 1994–95	$18.00	C126
☐ Arizona 1993–94	$18.00	C101	☐ New England 1994 (Avail. 1/94)	$16.00	C137
☐ Australia 1992–93	$18.00	C002	☐ New Mexico 1993–94	$15.00	C117
☐ Austria 1993–94	$19.00	C119	☐ New York State 1994–95	$19.00	C133
☐ Bahamas 1994–95	$17.00	C121	☐ Northwest 1994–95 (Avail. 2/94)	$17.00	C140
☐ Belgium/Holland/Luxembourg 1993–94	$18.00	C106	☐ Portugal 1994–95 (Avail. 2/94)	$17.00	C141
☐ Bermuda 1994–95	$15.00	C122	☐ Puerto Rico 1993–94	$15.00	C103
☐ Brazil 1993–94	$20.00	C111	☐ Puerto Vallarta/Manzanillo/Guadalajara 1994–95	$14.00	C028
☐ California 1994	$15.00	C134	☐ Scandinavia 1993–94	$19.00	C135
☐ Canada 1994–95 (Avail. 4/94)	$19.00	C145	☐ Scotland 1994–95 (Avail. 4/94)	$17.00	C146
☐ Caribbean 1994	$18.00	C123	☐ South Pacific 1994–95 (Avail. 1/94)	$20.00	C138
☐ Carolinas/Georgia 1994–95	$17.00	C128	☐ Spain 1993–94	$19.00	C115
☐ Colorado 1994–95 (Avail. 3/94)	$16.00	C143	☐ Switzerland/Liechtenstein 1994–95 (Avail. 1/94)	$19.00	C139
☐ Cruises 1993–94	$19.00	C107	☐ Thailand 1992–93	$20.00	C033
☐ Delaware/Maryland 1994–95 (Avail. 1/94)	$15.00	C136	☐ U.S.A. 1993–94	$19.00	C116
☐ England 1994	$18.00	C129	☐ Virgin Islands 1994–95	$13.00	C127
☐ Florida 1994	$18.00	C124	☐ Virginia 1994–95 (Avail. 2/94)	$14.00	C142
☐ France 1994–95	$20.00	C132	☐ Yucatán 1993–94	$18.00	C110
☐ Germany 1994	$19.00	C125			
☐ Italy 1994	$19.00	C130			
☐ Jamaica/Barbados 1993–94	$15.00	C105			
☐ Japan 1994–95 (Avail. 3/94)	$19.00	C144			

FROMMER'S $-A-DAY GUIDES
(Guides to low-cost tourist accommodations and facilities)

	Retail Price	Code		Retail Price	Code
☐ Australia on $45 1993–94	$18.00	D102	☐ Israel on $45 1993–94	$18.00	D101
☐ Costa Rica/Guatemala/Belize on $35 1993–94	$17.00	D108	☐ Mexico on $45 1994	$19.00	D116
☐ Eastern Europe on $30 1993–94	$18.00	D110	☐ New York on $70 1994–95	$16.00	D120
☐ England on $60 1994	$18.00	D112	☐ New Zealand on $45 1993–94	$18.00	D103
☐ Europe on $50 1994	$19.00	D115	☐ Scotland/Wales on $50 1992–93	$18.00	D019
☐ Greece on $45 1993–94	$19.00	D100	☐ South America on $40 1993–94	$19.00	D109
☐ Hawaii on $75 1994	$19.00	D113	☐ Turkey on $40 1992–93	$22.00	D023
☐ India on $40 1992–93	$20.00	D010	☐ Washington, D.C. on $40 1994–95 (Avail. 2/94)	$17.00	D119
☐ Ireland on $45 1994–95 (Avail. 1/94)	$17.00	D117			

FROMMER'S CITY $-A-DAY GUIDES
(Pocket-size guides to low-cost tourist accommodations and facilities)

	Retail Price	Code		Retail Price	Code
☐ Berlin on $40 1994–95	$12.00	D111	☐ Madrid on $50 1994–95 (Avail. 1/94)	$13.00	D118
☐ Copenhagen on $50 1992–93	$12.00	D003	☐ Paris on $50 1994–95	$12.00	D117
☐ London on $45 1994–95	$12.00	D114	☐ Stockholm on $50 1992–93	$13.00	D022

FROMMER'S WALKING TOURS
(With routes and detailed maps, these companion guides point out the places and pleasures that make a city unique)

	Retail Price	Code		Retail Price	Code
☐ Berlin	$12.00	W100	☐ Paris	$12.00	W103
☐ London	$12.00	W101	☐ San Francisco	$12.00	W104
☐ New York	$12.00	W102	☐ Washington, D.C.	$12.00	W105

FROMMER'S TOURING GUIDES
(Color-illustrated guides that include walking tours, cultural and historic sights, and practical information)

	Retail Price	Code		Retail Price	Code
☐ Amsterdam	$11.00	T001	☐ New York	$11.00	T008
☐ Barcelona	$14.00	T015	☐ Rome	$11.00	T010
☐ Brazil	$11.00	T003	☐ Scotland	$10.00	T011
☐ Florence	$ 9.00	T005	☐ Sicily	$15.00	T017
☐ Hong Kong/Singapore/			☐ Tokyo	$15.00	T016
Macau	$11.00	T006	☐ Turkey	$11.00	T013
☐ Kenya	$14.00	T018	☐ Venice	$ 9.00	T014
☐ London	$13.00	T007			

FROMMER'S FAMILY GUIDES

	Retail Price	Code		Retail Price	Code
☐ California with Kids	$18.00	F100	☐ San Francisco with Kids		
☐ Los Angeles with Kids			(Avail. 4/94)	$17.00	F104
(Avail. 4/94)	$17.00	F103	☐ Washington, D.C. with		
☐ New York City with Kids			Kids (Avail. 2/94)	$17.00	F102
(Avail. 2/94)	$18.00	F101			

FROMMER'S CITY GUIDES
(Pocket-size guides to sightseeing and tourist accommodations and facilities in all price ranges)

	Retail Price	Code		Retail Price	Code
☐ Amsterdam 1993–94	$13.00	S110	☐ Montréal/Québec		
☐ Athens 1993–94	$13.00	S114	City 1993–94	$13.00	S125
☐ Atlanta 1993–94	$13.00	S112	☐ Nashville/Memphis		
☐ Atlantic City/Cape			1994–95 (Avail. 4/94)	$13.00	S141
May 1993–94	$13.00	S130	☐ New Orleans 1993–		
☐ Bangkok 1992–93	$13.00	S005	94	$13.00	S103
☐ Barcelona/Majorca/			☐ New York 1994 (Avail.		
Minorca/Ibiza 1993–			1/94)	$13.00	S138
94	$13.00	S115	☐ Orlando 1994	$13.00	S135
☐ Berlin 1993–94	$13.00	S116	☐ Paris 1993–94	$13.00	S109
☐ Boston 1993–94	$13.00	S117	☐ Philadelphia 1993–94	$13.00	S113
☐ Budapest 1994–95			☐ San Diego 1993–94	$13.00	S107
(Avail. 2/94)	$13.00	S139	☐ San Francisco 1994	$13.00	S133
☐ Chicago 1993–94	$13.00	S122	☐ Santa Fe/Taos/		
☐ Denver/Boulder/			Albuquerque 1993–94	$13.00	S108
Colorado Springs			☐ Seattle/Portland 1994–		
1993–94	$13.00	S131	95	$13.00	S137
☐ Dublin 1993–94	$13.00	S128	☐ St. Louis/Kansas		
☐ Hong Kong 1994–95			City 1993–94	$13.00	S127
(Avail. 4/94)	$13.00	S140	☐ Sydney 1993–94	$13.00	S129
☐ Honolulu/Oahu 1994	$13.00	S134	☐ Tampa/St.		
☐ Las Vegas 1993–94	$13.00	S121	Petersburg 1993–94	$13.00	S105
☐ London 1993–94	$13.00	S132	☐ Tokyo 1992–93	$13.00	S039
☐ Los Angeles 1993–94	$13.00	S123	☐ Toronto 1993–94	$13.00	S126
☐ Madrid/Costa del			☐ Vancouver/Victoria		
Sol 1993–94	$13.00	S124	1994–95 (Avail. 1/94)	$13.00	S142
☐ Miami 1993–94	$13.00	S118	☐ Washington,		
☐ Minneapolis/St.			D.C. 1994 (Avail.		
Paul 1993–94	$13.00	S119	1/94)	$13.00	S136

SPECIAL EDITIONS

	Retail Price	Code		Retail Price	Code
☐ Bed & Breakfast Southwest	$16.00	P100	☐ Caribbean Hideaways	$16.00	P103
☐ Bed & Breakfast Great American Cities (Avail. 1/94)	$16.00	P104	☐ National Park Guide 1994 (Avail. 3/94)	$16.00	P105
			☐ Where to Stay U.S.A.	$15.00	P102

Please note: if the availability of a book is several months away, we may have back issues of guides to that particular destination. Call customer service at (815) 734-1104.